GENERATION Z, EMPOWERING ANXIOUS GENERATION

Strategies for a Resilient Anxious Generation

Raquel Williams

Scan me for more books from Raquel Williams

Table of Contents

Introduction to Generation Z

In the ever-evolving landscape of the 21st century, Generation Z stands as a unique cohort, born into a world of rapid technological advancements, unprecedented social change, and mounting global challenges. As the first true digital natives, Gen Z navigates a complex terrain where the lines between the virtual and the real are increasingly blurred. While this generation exhibits remarkable adaptability and potential, it also faces an alarming rise in anxiety and mental health issues that threaten to undermine its promise.

Recent studies and surveys reveal a stark reality: Generation Z is grappling with anxiety and mental health challenges at unprecedented levels. The constant barrage of information, societal pressures, and the relentless pursuit of success in an increasingly competitive world have contributed to an environment where stress and anxiety are pervasive. The COVID-19 pandemic further exacerbated these issues, highlighting the critical need for effective strategies to support the mental well-being of this generation.

"Generation Z, Empowering Anxious Generation" is not just another book on mental health. It is a comprehensive guide designed to address the unique challenges faced by Gen Z, offering practical, evidence-based strategies to foster resilience and empower this anxious generation. Whether you are a member of Gen Z, a parent, an educator, or a mental health professional, this book provides valuable insights and actionable advice to help you understand and support the journey toward mental well-being.

This book is divided into ten chapters, each meticulously crafted to cover essential aspects of mental health and resilience. We start by understanding the distinct characteristics and challenges of Generation Z, followed by an exploration of the root causes of their anxiety. The subsequent chapters offer practical strategies for building resilience, managing mental health, and maintaining physical well-being. We also delve into the critical areas of education, career planning, and the impact of digital life, providing holistic guidance for a balanced and fulfilling life.

Each chapter includes:
In-Depth Analysis: Comprehensive insights into the factors contributing to anxiety and mental health challenges.

Practical Strategies: Step-by-step techniques and approaches to build resilience and manage stress.
Real-Life Examples: Stories and case studies that illustrate the application of these strategies.
Actionable Exercises: Activities and worksheets to help you implement the concepts in your daily life.

At the heart of this book is a message of empowerment. Generation Z has the potential to become one of the most resilient and innovative generations in history. This book is a call to action for everyone invested in the future of our youth to come together and create a supportive environment that fosters mental well-being and resilience.

Join us on this journey to empower an anxious generation and build a future where mental health is prioritised, resilience is cultivated, and every member of Generation Z can thrive.

The Urgency of Addressing Gen Z's Mental Health

Generation Z, comprising individuals born roughly between the mid-1990s and early 2010s, is navigating a world vastly different from that of previous generations. The rapid pace of technological advancement, coupled with significant societal shifts and unprecedented global challenges, has placed unique pressures on this cohort. Understanding the urgency of addressing Gen Z's mental health is important for several compelling reasons:

1. Epidemic Levels of Anxiety and Depression

Recent statistics paint a concerning picture: anxiety and depression rates among Generation Z are higher than any other age group. According to the American Psychological Association, Gen Z reports the highest levels of stress and mental health issues. Factors contributing to this include academic pressures, economic uncertainty, social media influence, and global issues like climate change and political instability. Ignoring these mental health crises risks long-term consequences not only for individuals but for society at large.

2. The Impact of Social Media and Technology

Generation Z is the first generation to grow up with smartphones and social media as integral parts of daily life. While these technologies offer numerous benefits, they also contribute significantly to anxiety and depression. The constant comparison, cyberbullying, and the pressure to maintain a perfect online persona can lead to feelings of inadequacy and chronic stress. Addressing these issues is crucial to mitigating their negative impact on mental health.

3. Academic and Career Pressures

The modern educational landscape and job market are intensely competitive. From a young age, Gen Z faces immense pressure to excel academically and secure a stable, well-paying job. This relentless pursuit of success can lead to burnout and severe anxiety. Additionally, the uncertainty of the future job market, exacerbated by rapid technological changes and economic volatility, adds to their stress. Providing strategies to manage these pressures is essential for fostering a healthier, more balanced approach to education and career planning.

4. Global Challenges and Their Psychological Impact

Generation Z is acutely aware of global issues such as climate change, political instability, and social injustice. This heightened awareness, while leading to increased activism and engagement, also contributes to a sense of existential dread and helplessness. The psychological toll of these global challenges cannot be underestimated. Addressing mental health in this context involves empowering

Gen Z with resilience-building tools to cope with and contribute positively to these global challenges.

5. The Long-Term Societal Implications

The mental health of Generation Z has far-reaching implications for society. Poor mental health can lead to decreased productivity, higher healthcare costs, and a greater burden on social support systems. Conversely, a mentally healthy and resilient Generation Z can drive innovation, economic growth, and societal well-being. Investing in the mental health of this generation is not just a moral imperative but a strategic one for the future prosperity and stability of our communities.

6. Creating a Supportive Ecosystem

Addressing Gen Z's mental health requires a multifaceted approach that involves parents, educators, employers, policymakers, and mental health professionals. It calls for creating an ecosystem that promotes mental well-being through supportive relationships, accessible resources, and an open dialogue about mental health. By fostering a supportive environment, we can help Generation Z thrive despite the challenges they face.

The urgency of addressing Generation Z's mental health is clear. By understanding the unique pressures they face and implementing targeted strategies to support their well-being, we can empower this generation to overcome anxiety, build resilience, and reach their full potential. "Generation Z, Empowering Anxious Generation" aims to provide the tools and insights needed to achieve this goal, fostering a future where mental health is prioritised and every member of Generation Z can thrive.

Why This Book Matters

"Generation Z, Empowering Anxious Generation" is not just another book on mental health; it is a crucial resource designed to address the specific needs of Generation Z. Here's why this book is significant and how it stands out in a crowded field.

1. Tailored to a Unique Generation: Generation Z faces unique challenges that differ significantly from those encountered by previous generations. Born into a digital world, they have grown up with constant connectivity, social media pressures, and a rapidly changing socio-economic landscape. This book specifically addresses these contemporary issues, providing insights and solutions tailored to their experiences. By focusing on Gen Z, this book ensures relevance and relatability, making it a vital tool for understanding and supporting this generation.

2. Comprehensive and Holistic Approach: This book takes a comprehensive approach, covering a wide range of topics from understanding the roots of anxiety to practical strategies for building resilience. It integrates various aspects of life, including education, career planning, physical health, and digital detox, ensuring a holistic understanding and approach to mental wellness. Readers will find valuable guidance that addresses all dimensions of their lives.

3. Evidence-Based Strategies: In an era where misinformation can spread rapidly, this book stands out by grounding its advice in evidence-based strategies. The techniques and approaches recommended are backed by scientific research and clinical expertise. By providing reliable, proven methods for managing anxiety and building resilience, the book ensures that readers can trust and effectively implement the strategies discussed.

4. Actionable Advice and Practical Tools: One of the key strengths of this book is its emphasis on actionable advice. Each chapter is designed not only to inform but also to empower readers with practical tools and techniques they can apply in their daily lives. From mindfulness exercises to stress management techniques, the book offers a wealth of practical resources. Worksheets and exercises included in the appendices provide a hands-on approach to self-improvement and mental health maintenance.

5. Inspiring Real-Life Examples Stories and case studies of real people provide powerful illustrations of the concepts discussed. These narratives make the theoretical content more relatable and demonstrate the effectiveness of the strategies in real-life situations. By showcasing the journeys of others who have successfully navigated similar challenges, the book offers inspiration and hope, showing readers that they are not alone and that change is possible.

6. Creating a Supportive Community: Mental health challenges can often feel isolating. This book emphasises the importance of building and leveraging support networks, including family, friends, educators, and mental health professionals. It encourages open dialogue about mental health, breaking down the stigma that often surrounds these issues.

7. Preparing for Future Challenge: The landscape of the future is unpredictable, with rapid technological advancements and global challenges continuously reshaping our world. This book prepares Generation Z to adapt to these changes by fostering resilience and a growth mindset. It provides strategies for long-term mental health and equips readers with the skills needed to navigate future uncertainties confidently.

How to Use This Book

"Generation Z, Empowering Anxious Generation" is designed to be a comprehensive guide for understanding and addressing the mental health challenges faced by Generation Z. To maximize the benefits of this book, here is a detailed and powerful explanation of how to use it effectively:

1. Start with the Introduction:

The introduction sets the stage for the entire book, providing context and outlining the urgency of addressing Gen Z's mental health. By starting here, you will gain a foundational understanding of why this book is essential and what it aims to achieve. It will also give you a clear sense of the book's structure and how each chapter builds upon the previous one.

2. Read Sequentially or Jump to Relevant Sections:

While the book is structured to build knowledge progressively, you can also jump directly to sections that are most relevant to your immediate needs. Each chapter is designed to stand alone, offering valuable insights and strategies on specific topics. Whether you are dealing with academic pressures, social media stress, or seeking to build resilience, you can find the guidance you need in the corresponding chapter.

3. Engage with the In-Depth Analysis:

Each chapter begins with an in-depth analysis of the topic at hand. This analysis provides a thorough understanding of the issue, backed by current research and statistics. Engaging with this content will help you grasp the complexities of the challenges Generation Z faces and the underlying factors contributing to these issues. A solid understanding is crucial for effectively implementing the strategies that follow.

4. Apply Practical Strategies:

The heart of each chapter lies in the practical strategies provided. These strategies are evidence-based and designed to be easily implemented in daily life. Take the time to read through these sections carefully, and consider how each strategy can be adapted to your specific circumstances. Whether it's a mindfulness exercise, a stress management technique, or advice on building healthy digital habits, these strategies are your tools for creating positive change.

5. Utilize Real-Life Examples:

Real-life examples and case studies are included to illustrate the application of strategies in real-world scenarios. These examples provide inspiration and show that overcoming mental health challenges is possible. Reflect on these stories and consider how the individuals' experiences resonate with your own. This can help you feel less isolated in your journey and more confident in applying the strategies to your life.

6. Complete the Actionable Exercises:

At the end of each chapter, you will find actionable exercises and worksheets. These are designed to reinforce the concepts discussed and provide a hands-on approach to implementing the strategies. Completing these exercises will help you internalise the lessons and track your progress. They also offer a practical way to reflect on your experiences and plan for future improvements.

7. Create a Support Network:

Building a supportive environment is a key theme throughout the book. Use the guidance provided to reach out to family, friends, educators, and mental health professionals. Discuss the concepts and strategies from the book with them, and work together to create a supportive network. This collaborative approach can significantly enhance the effectiveness of the strategies and provide ongoing support.

8. Reflect and Revisit:

Mental health and resilience-building are ongoing processes. Periodically revisit chapters and exercises as you continue on your journey. Reflect on your progress, adjust strategies as needed, and celebrate your successes. The book is designed to be a long-term resource, offering value every time you return to it.

9. Utilise the Appendices

The appendices provide additional resources, including further reading, helpful organisations, and additional worksheets. These resources can offer deeper insights and further support your journey. Make use of these supplementary materials to expand your knowledge and access additional tools.

"Generation Z, Empowering Anxious Generation" is more than just a book; it is a toolkit for navigating the complexities of modern life with resilience and confidence. By engaging fully with each section, applying the practical strategies, and leveraging the support network around you, you can transform anxiety into empowerment. This book is your companion on the journey to mental well-being, offering guidance, inspiration, and practical tools every step of the way.

Chapter 1

1.0 Who is Generation Z

Generation Z, also known as Gen Z, iGen, or Post-Millennials, is the demographic cohort born roughly between the mid-to-late 1990s and the early 2010s. The exact birth years vary depending on the source, but they are typically defined as those born from 1997 to 2012. This generation succeeds Millennials (also known as Generation Y) and precedes Generation Alpha.

Characteristics of Generation Z:

1. Digital Natives: Gen Z is the first generation to grow up entirely in the digital age, with smartphones, social media, and the internet shaping their daily experiences and interactions.

2. Diverse and Inclusive: This generation is the most diverse in terms of ethnicity, race, and cultural background. They prioritise inclusivity and are more likely to support social justice causes such as LGBTQ+ rights and racial equality.

3. Global Connectivity: Gen Z is globally connected through digital platforms, allowing them to access information, communicate across borders, and engage in global issues like climate change and human rights.

4. Pragmatic and Financially Cautious: Having witnessed economic downturns like the 2008 financial crisis and the COVID-19 pandemic, Gen Z tends to prioritise financial stability and practical career choices.

5. Mental Health Awareness: Compared to previous generations, Gen Z is more open about discussing mental health issues and seeks resources and support more readily.

6. Education and Learning Preferences: They value flexible, digital learning environments and are comfortable with online education platforms and collaborative tools.

7. Entrepreneurial and Innovative: Many Gen Z individuals are entrepreneurial-minded, leveraging digital tools to create content, start businesses, and pursue freelance opportunities.

Understanding who Generation Z is involves recognizing their unique characteristics, experiences, and perspectives shaped by growing up in a rapidly evolving digital and social landscape.

1.1 Defining Gen Z: Characteristics and Traits

Generation Z, born roughly between the mid-1990s and early 2010s, is the first generation to grow up in a world where the internet and digital technology are omnipresent. Understanding the defining characteristics and traits of this generation is important for addressing their unique challenges and empowering them effectively.

Here is a detailed and powerful explanation of who Gen Z is and what sets them apart:

1. Digital Natives:

Generation Z is the first true digital-native generation. They have never known a world without the internet, smartphones, and social media. This constant connectivity shapes their communication styles, social interactions, and access to information. Unlike previous generations, Gen Z seamlessly integrates digital tools into every aspect of their lives, from education and entertainment to socialisation and activism.

Implications: Their digital fluency means they are quick to adapt to new technologies and platforms, making them highly adaptable and tech-savvy. However, this also exposes them to unique challenges such as cyberbullying, digital addiction, and the pressure to maintain a perfect online persona.

2. Highly Educated and Informed:

Gen Z has unprecedented access to information. The internet provides them with a wealth of knowledge at their fingertips, leading to a generation that is highly informed about global issues, social justice, and current events. This access to information fosters a sense of awareness and activism, as many Gen Zers are deeply involved in social and environmental causes.

Implications: Their awareness and engagement with global issues drive them to be socially and environmentally conscious consumers and citizens. However, the constant stream of information can also contribute to anxiety and information overload.

3. Diverse and Inclusive:

Generation Z is the most diverse generation in history, with a significant representation of different ethnicities, cultures, and identities. This diversity extends to their values, as they tend to prioritize inclusivity and equality. They are more likely to embrace and advocate for LGBTQ+ rights, gender equality, and racial justice.

Implications: This generation's commitment to diversity and inclusion makes them progressive and open-minded, often leading societal change. However, they may also experience stress and frustration when confronted with persistent inequalities and injustices.

4. Pragmatic and Financially Cautious:

Having witnessed the economic turmoil of the 2008 financial crisis and the impact of the COVID-19 pandemic, Gen Z tends to be pragmatic and financially cautious. They are more likely to value stability and security, often prioritising practical career choices and financial planning.

Implications: Their financial pragmatism drives them to seek out stable career paths and be savvy consumers. However, this caution can also manifest as anxiety about future job prospects and economic stability.

5. Mental Health Awareness:

Generation Z is more open about discussing mental health than previous generations. They recognize the importance of mental well-being and are more likely to seek help for mental health issues. This openness is partly due to the increased visibility of mental health discussions on social media and the destigmatization of seeking therapy.

Implications: Their awareness and openness about mental health can lead to more proactive and effective management of mental health issues. However, the high prevalence of anxiety and depression in this generation indicates a need for robust mental health support systems.

6. Preference for Authenticity:

Gen Z values authenticity and transparency. They are sceptical of traditional advertising and prefer brands, influencers, and leaders who are genuine and transparent. They are drawn to content that feels real and relatable, often favouring raw and unfiltered over polished and perfect.

Implications: Brands and organisations that engage authentically with Gen Z can build strong, loyal relationships. On the flip side, they are quick to call out and disengage from entities that they perceive as inauthentic or deceptive.

7. Collaborative and Entrepreneurial Spirit

Many Gen Zers possess a collaborative and entrepreneurial spirit. They are comfortable working in teams, often leveraging digital tools for remote collaboration. Additionally, a significant number of them aspire to start their own businesses or engage in freelance work, driven by the desire for autonomy and creativity.

Implications: This entrepreneurial mindset makes Gen Z innovative and resourceful, well-suited for the gig economy and startup culture. However, the pursuit of entrepreneurial ventures can also come with stress and uncertainty.

Understanding the defining characteristics and traits of Generation Z is essential for effectively addressing their needs and harnessing their potential. By recognizing their digital fluency, diversity, financial pragmatism, mental health awareness, preference for authenticity, and entrepreneurial spirit, we can develop strategies that empower and support this generation. "Generation Z, Empowering Anxious Generation" provides the tools and insights needed to navigate the complexities of modern life, helping Gen Z thrive in an ever-changing world.

1.2. Growing Up in a Digital Age

This unique upbringing has profoundly shaped their worldview, behaviours, and mental health. Understanding the implications of growing up with constant connectivity and digital immersion is crucial for supporting and empowering this generation. Here's a detailed explanation of the impact of the digital age on Gen Z.

1. Ubiquitous Connectivity:

From a young age, Gen Z has been surrounded by digital devices and the internet. Smartphones, tablets, and computers are integral parts of their daily lives, providing instant access to information, entertainment, and communication. This constant connectivity has created a generation that is always online and always connected.

Implications: The ability to stay connected offers numerous benefits, such as easy access to educational resources, global communication, and social interaction. However, it also leads to challenges like digital addiction, where the need to be constantly online can interfere with sleep, productivity, and face-to-face relationships.

2. Social Media Influence:

Social media platforms like Instagram, TikTok, Snapchat, and YouTube are central to Gen Z's social lives. These platforms influence how they communicate, form relationships, and perceive themselves and the world around them. Social media provides a space for self-expression, creativity, and connection but also exposes users to cyberbullying, unrealistic comparisons, and peer pressure.

Implications: While social media can foster a sense of community and belonging, it can also contribute to anxiety, depression, and low self-esteem. The pressure to present a curated and idealized version of oneself can lead to feelings of inadequacy and stress. It is crucial to help Gen Z develop healthy social media habits and resilience against negative online influences.

3. Instant Gratification and Short Attention Spans:

The digital age has fostered a culture of instant gratification, where information, entertainment, and social interaction are just a click away. This has shaped Gen Z's expectations for immediate responses and quick results. As a result, their attention spans are shorter, and they may struggle with activities requiring prolonged focus and patience.

Implications: The preference for instant gratification can impact academic performance and job satisfaction, as tasks that require sustained effort and delayed rewards may be less appealing. Strategies to build focus and patience, such as mindfulness and time management techniques, are essential for helping Gen Z navigate these challenges.

4. Digital Learning and Education:

Gen Z's educational experiences are heavily influenced by digital technologies. Online learning platforms, virtual classrooms, and digital resources are commonplace. This shift has made education more accessible and customizable, allowing students to learn at their own pace and explore a wide range of subjects.

Implications: While digital learning offers flexibility and access to vast resources, it also presents challenges such as digital distractions, the digital divide, and the need for self-discipline. Ensuring that Gen Z can effectively leverage digital tools for learning while maintaining focus and motivation is crucial for their educational success.

5. Cybersecurity and Privacy Concerns:

Growing up in a digital age means that Gen Z is more aware of cybersecurity and privacy issues. They understand the importance of protecting personal information online but also face the challenge of navigating complex digital landscapes where data breaches and cyber threats are common.

Implications: Educating Gen Z about digital literacy, cybersecurity, and privacy protection is essential. They need to be equipped with the knowledge and skills to safeguard their digital identities and make informed decisions about their online activities.

6. The Role of Digital Creators and Influencers:

Digital platforms have democratised content creation, allowing Gen Z to become creators and influencers. Many young people are building personal brands, creating content, and even generating income through social media. This trend has opened up new career opportunities and avenues for self-expression.

Implications: While being a digital creator can be empowering and lucrative, it also comes with pressures and risks, such as maintaining an audience, dealing with negative feedback, and balancing online and offline life. Supporting Gen Z in navigating these opportunities responsibly is crucial for their well-being.

Growing up in a digital age has fundamentally shaped Generation Z, bringing both opportunities and challenges. Understanding the impact of constant connectivity, social media influence, instant gratification, digital learning, cybersecurity concerns, and the role of digital creators is essential for providing the support and guidance they need. "Generation Z, Empowering Anxious Generation" delves into these aspects, offering practical strategies to help Gen Z navigate their digital world healthily and effectively, ensuring they can thrive both online and offline.

1.3. The Social and Cultural Landscape

Generation Z's formative years have been shaped by a complex and rapidly evolving social and cultural landscape. This environment has influenced their values, behaviours, and perspectives in profound ways. To effectively support and empower Gen Z, it's crucial to understand the key elements of the social and cultural context in which they are growing up. Here's a explanation of the factors that define this landscape:

1. Diversity and Inclusion

Generation Z is the most diverse generation in history, growing up in a world where multiculturalism is the norm. They value diversity in all its forms, including race, ethnicity, gender, sexuality, and ability. Inclusivity is a core principle for Gen Z, and they are vocal advocates for equality and social justice.

Implications: This generation's commitment to diversity and inclusion shapes their social interactions, consumer behaviours, and career choices. Organisations and brands that prioritise diversity and inclusion resonate more with Gen Z. However, their heightened awareness also means they are critical of superficial or performative efforts at inclusivity.

2. Social Justice and Activism:

Gen Z is deeply engaged in social justice issues. They have been at the forefront of movements advocating for climate action, racial equality, gender rights, and more. This activism is often fueled by their access to information and the organisational power of social media.

Implications: Gen Z's activism drives them to seek out and support brands, organisations, and leaders who align with their values. However, the constant exposure to social justice issues can also lead to activism fatigue and a sense of overwhelming responsibility. It's important to provide tools for sustainable activism and self-care.

3. Global Connectivity:

The internet and social media have made Gen Z more globally connected than any previous generation. They are exposed to diverse cultures, ideas, and perspectives from around the world, leading to a broader worldview and a stronger sense of global citizenship.

Implications: This global perspective encourages Gen Z to think beyond local and national boundaries, fostering a sense of empathy and solidarity with people from different backgrounds. However, it also means they are more aware of global crises and injustices, which can contribute to anxiety and a feeling of helplessness.

4. Evolving Family Dynamics:

Gen Z is growing up in a time of changing family structures and dynamics. Increased acceptance of diverse family forms, such as single-parent families, blended families, and LGBTQ+ families, is reshaping traditional notions of family life.

Implications: These evolving dynamics influence Gen Z's understanding of relationships, support systems, and identity. They are likely to be more accepting and adaptable in their personal lives. However, navigating these changes can also present emotional and psychological challenges.

5. Mental Health Awareness:

There is a growing recognition of mental health issues within Gen Z. They are more open to discussing mental health and seeking help compared to previous generations. This openness is partly driven by social media campaigns and public figures who advocate for mental health awareness.

Implications: The increased focus on mental health can lead to better outcomes as Gen Z is more likely to seek support and practice self-care. However, the prevalence of anxiety and depression highlights the need for accessible mental health resources and effective coping strategies.

6. Economic Uncertainty:

Gen Z has been shaped by economic events like the 2008 financial crisis and the economic impact of the COVID-19 pandemic. These experiences have made them financially cautious and pragmatic, often prioritising stability and security in their career and financial planning.

Implications: This financial prudence drives Gen Z to be more cautious consumers and thoughtful about their career choices. However, economic uncertainty also contributes to stress and anxiety about the future, underscoring the need for financial education and support.

7. Technology and Innovation:

Technological innovation is a constant in the lives of Gen Z. From AI and automation to the gig economy and remote work, technological advancements are continuously reshaping the social and cultural landscape.

Implications: Gen Z's comfort with technology makes them adaptable and innovative, well-suited for the modern workforce. However, the fast pace of technological change also means they must continually update their skills and navigate new forms of digital interaction and collaboration.

The social and cultural landscape that shapes Generation Z is characterised by diversity, social justice, global connectivity, evolving family dynamics, mental health awareness, economic uncertainty, and technological innovation. Understanding these factors is essential for providing the support and resources Gen Z needs to thrive. "Generation Z, Empowering Anxious Generation" offers comprehensive insights and practical strategies to navigate this complex landscape, empowering Gen Z to build a resilient and fulfilling future.

1.4. Key Differences from Previous Generations

Generation Z, born between the mid-1990s and early 2010s, exhibits several distinct characteristics and experiences that set them apart from previous generations. Understanding these differences is essential for effectively supporting and engaging with Gen Z. Here are the key contrasts between Generation Z and previous generations:

1. Digital Natives vs. Digital Immigrants:

They are digital natives, meaning they have been exposed to digital technologies like smartphones, social media, and the internet from a young age. In contrast, previous generations, such as Millennials (Gen Y) and Generation X, experienced the transition to digital technologies later in life.

Implications: Gen Z's digital fluency and comfort with technology influence how they communicate, learn, work, and socialise. They expect instant access to information and are adept at navigating online platforms. This digital upbringing has also shaped their worldview and preferences in entertainment, education, and social interactions.

2. Diverse and Inclusive Values:

Generation Z is characterised by its embrace of diversity and inclusivity. They are the most ethnically and racially diverse generation in history and are more likely to support LGBTQ+ rights, gender equality, and racial justice compared to previous generations. This commitment to diversity is reflected in their social interactions, consumer behaviours, and political views.

Implications: Organisations and brands that prioritise diversity and inclusion resonate more with

Gen Z. They are vocal advocates for social justice issues and expect authenticity and transparency from institutions. This emphasis on inclusivity has reshaped societal norms and expectations, influencing everything from marketing strategies to workplace culture.

3. Economic Realities and Pragmatism:

Unlike Millennials who entered the workforce during economic prosperity, Generation Z has experienced economic uncertainty from an early age. They witnessed the impact of the 2008 financial crisis and the economic downturn caused by the COVID-19 pandemic, leading them to prioritise stability and financial security.

Implications: Gen Z tends to be financially cautious and pragmatic in their career choices and spending habits. They value job stability, seek practical skills for the modern economy, and are entrepreneurial-minded. This economic pragmatism contrasts with the more idealistic and adventurous approach often associated with Millennials.

4. Mental Health Awareness and Openness:

Generation Z exhibits a greater awareness and openness about mental health compared to previous generations. They are more likely to discuss mental health issues openly, seek professional help when needed, and prioritise self-care practices. This shift is partly due to increased visibility of mental health discussions on social media and efforts to destigmatize mental illness.

Implications: While Gen Z's openness about mental health is positive, they also face unique stressors such as academic pressures, social media comparisons, and global uncertainties. Addressing their mental health needs requires accessible resources, supportive environments, and strategies to build resilience against digital and societal pressures.

5. Global Connectivity and Activism:

Generation Z is globally connected like never before, thanks to the internet and social media. They are active participants in global conversations on social justice, climate change, and human rights. Social media platforms have amplified their voices, allowing them to mobilise and advocate for causes they care about.

Implications: Gen Z's activism spans local and global issues, influencing policy debates and corporate practices. They expect organisations to take a stand on social and environmental issues and support brands that align with their values. Their digital activism has reshaped traditional forms of advocacy and activism seen in previous generations.

6. Education and Learning Preferences

The educational experiences of Generation Z differ significantly from those of previous generations. They have grown up with digital learning tools, online resources, and personalised learning platforms. Gen Z values flexibility, customization, and practical application of knowledge in their education.

Implications: Traditional educational models may need to adapt to accommodate Gen Z's preferences for digital learning, collaborative projects, and real-world applications. They are adept at using technology for research, collaboration, and self-directed learning, influencing educational trends and innovations.

Generation Z stands out from previous generations in terms of their digital fluency, diverse and inclusive values, economic pragmatism, mental health awareness, global activism, and preferences in education. Understanding these key differences is essential for effectively engaging with and supporting Gen Z as they navigate a rapidly changing world. "Generation Z, Empowering Anxious Generation" provides insights and strategies to harness their strengths and empower them to thrive in today's society.

Chapter 2

2.0 The Rise of Anxiety

The rise of anxiety refers to the observed increase in the prevalence of anxiety disorders and anxiety-related symptoms in recent years. This phenomenon can be attributed to various factors, including societal changes, environmental influences, and advancements in mental health awareness.

Key Factors Contributing to the Rise of Anxiety:

1. Increased Stressors: Modern life often involves juggling multiple responsibilities, financial pressures, and societal expectations, leading to heightened stress levels that may contribute to anxiety.

2. Social Media and Technology: The prevalence of social media and digital communication can create a sense of constant connectedness, fostering feelings of pressure to maintain a certain image, fear of missing out, and cyberbullying, which can contribute to anxiety.

3. Societal Uncertainty: Rapid changes in the world, such as political unrest, economic instability, and global health crises, can create a sense of uncertainty and fear that may heighten anxiety.

4. **Workplace Pressure:** Increasing demands in the workplace, such as longer work hours, job insecurity, and the need to continuously acquire new skills, can contribute to anxiety.

5. **Environmental Factors:** Urbanisation, overcrowding, and pollution can create living conditions that may exacerbate anxiety.

6. **Genetics and Biology:** Anxiety disorders can have a genetic component, and individual differences in brain chemistry and functioning may contribute to increased susceptibility to anxiety.

For more Factors Influencing Anxiety consider this,

1. **Stress:** Stress is a major contributor. As economic uncertainty grows and the middle class erodes, anxiety becomes more common.

2. **Genetics and Environment:** A combination of genetic predisposition and environmental factors plays a role in anxiety disorders.

3. Brain Chemistry: Researchers study brain chemistry, particularly areas controlling fear responses, as a potential cause.

4. Media Exposure: Constant exposure to global events amplifies anxiety. We're more aware of crises, leading to increased reporting and awareness.

5. Academic and Economic Stress: Young adults face high stress levels due to academic pressures and economic challenges5.

Recent Trends in the U.S.:

2024 Poll Results: This information highlights a significant trend in the U.S. regarding the mental health of its population. The reported increase in anxiety levels from 32% in 2022 to 37% in 2023 and further to 43% in 2024 indicates a growing concern for the well-being of U.S. adults.

Several factors appear to be contributing to this rise in anxiety, including:

Stress and Sleep: Stress (53%) and sleep (40%) are key factors impacting mental health. Social connection matters more for younger adults

Seeking Help: Despite increasing anxiety, most adults haven't sought professional mental health support. Telehealth services are critical during the pandemic.

Consequences of the Rise in Anxiety:

1. Impaired Quality of Life: Anxiety can negatively impact an individual's overall well-being, leading to physical symptoms, social withdrawal, and difficulties in daily functioning.

2. Strain on Mental Health Services: The increased prevalence of anxiety has led to greater demand for mental health services, potentially straining available resources.

3. Economic Implications: Anxiety can lead to absenteeism from work, reduced productivity, and increased healthcare costs, resulting in significant economic burdens.

4. Intergenerational Effects: Anxiety can have long-lasting effects on children who grow up in anxious environments, potentially contributing to a cycle of anxiety across generations.

Addressing the rise of anxiety requires a comprehensive approach involving mental health awareness, education, early intervention, and improved access to effective treatments.

Encouraging open dialogue about mental health, fostering supportive communities, and implementing societal changes to alleviate stressors can help mitigate the impact of anxiety on individuals and society.

Global Trends in Anxiety

1. Prevalence Increase: Over the past decade, anxiety has become more prevalent worldwide1. The exact reasons are multifaceted, but several factors play a role.

2. COVID-19 Pandemic: The pandemic significantly impacted anxiety levels. Initially, anxiety rose due to fear of the unknown, lockdowns, and health concerns. However, it later decreased as people adapted.

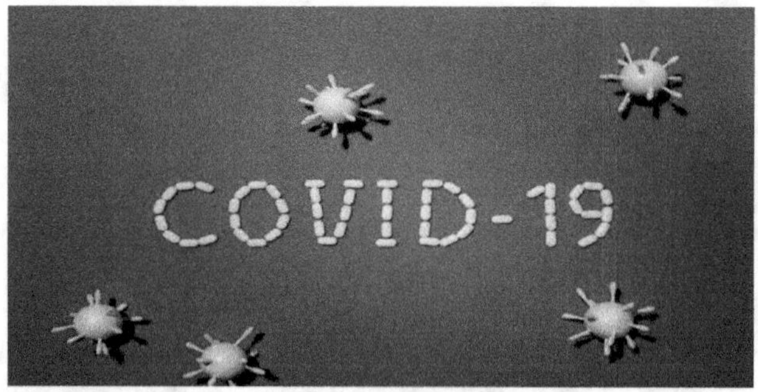

4. Economic and Political Factors: Beyond the pandemic, economic instability and political events also contribute to rising anxiety levels.

2.1. Understanding Anxiety in Gen Z

Understanding anxiety in Gen Z is important, as this generation faces unique challenges and stressors that can significantly impact their mental health. Born between the late 1990s and early 2010s, Gen Z has grown up in an era characterised by rapid technological advancements, political and social unrest, and economic uncertainty.

Key Aspects of Anxiety in Gen Z

1. Digital Natives: As the first generation to grow up entirely in the digital age, Gen Z's constant exposure to technology and social media can contribute to anxiety. Online pressures, cyberbullying, and the fear of missing out (FOMO) can exacerbate mental health concerns.

2. Societal Pressure: Social interactions have shifted online, but Gen Z still faces social anxiety. Fear of judgement, cyberbullying, and the pressure to curate a flawless online persona contribute to this. Building social skills, practising self-compassion, and seeking professional help if needed are important

.

3.Political and Social Unrest: Growing up amidst political turmoil, global conflicts, and heightened awareness of social injustices can create an environment of stress and anxiety for Gen Z.

4. Economic Uncertainty: Gen Z witnessed economic recessions, student loan debt, and job market volatility. Financial stress impacts mental health. Teaching financial literacy, encouraging entrepreneurship, and fostering resilience can mitigate anxiety. Financial instability and growing economic inequality can exacerbate anxiety among Gen Z as they navigate their futures and strive for financial security.

Consider this for more of Key Aspects of Anxiety in Gen Z

1. Academic Pressure: Gen Z experiences intense academic pressure. High-stakes exams, college admissions, and the pursuit of perfection can lead to stress and anxiety. Encouraging a growth mindset, emphasising learning over grades, and seeking support when needed are essential.

2. Climate Change Anxiety: Gen Z is passionate about environmental issues. Climate change, natural disasters, and eco-anxiety weigh heavily on their minds. Empowering them to take action, promoting eco-friendly habits, and emphasising collective efforts can alleviate anxiety.

3. Self-Care and Coping Strategies: Encourage mindfulness, physical activity, creative outlets, and healthy coping mechanisms. Gen Z can benefit from meditation apps, journaling, and connecting with nature.

Strategies to Support Gen Z

1. Access to Mental Health Services: Improving access to affordable, high-quality mental health services, including therapy and counselling, can help Gen Z address anxiety and develop healthy coping mechanisms.

2. Education and Awareness: Schools, families, and communities can work together to promote mental health awareness and education, reducing the stigma surrounding anxiety and other mental health issues.

3. Technology and Social Media Management: Encouraging healthy digital habits, such as limiting screen time and promoting digital detoxes, can help alleviate anxiety related to technology and social media use.

4. Supportive Environments: Creating safe, inclusive spaces in schools, workplaces, and communities can help Gen Z feel supported as they navigate life's challenges and uncertainties.

5. **Mentorship and Guidance:** Providing Gen Z with access to mentorship and guidance from older generations can offer valuable support and perspective as they make decisions about their futures.

Resilience isn't about avoiding stress—it's about bouncing back and growing stronger. Gen Z has immense potential to thrive with the right tools and support.

2.2. The Role of Social Media

Social media plays a significant role in the rise of anxiety, particularly among Gen Z. With its widespread adoption and integration into daily life, social media has created new platforms for communication, information sharing, and self-expression. However, it also brings challenges that can negatively impact mental health.

Factors Linking Social Media and Anxiety:

1. Constant Connectivity: The always-on nature of social media can create a feeling of constant connection that makes it difficult to disconnect and relax, leading to increased anxiety.

2. Fear of Missing Out (FOMO): Social media constantly updates users on events, parties, and gatherings. Gen Z may experience FOMO if they miss out on social activities, leading to anxiety and a sense of exclusion. Seeing friends' posts about events or experiences can trigger FOMO and feelings of exclusion, contributing to anxiety and low self-esteem.

3. Comparison and Idealised Lives: Many people present idealised versions of their lives on social media, leading others to compare themselves unfavourably to these curated portrayals and feel inadequate or anxious about their lives.

4. Cyberbullying and Trolling: Social media can be a platform for cyberbullying, which can cause significant anxiety and emotional distress. Online spaces aren't always kind. Cyberbullying, negative comments, and trolling can harm mental health. Gen Z faces these challenges, impacting their self-esteem and overall well-being.

5. News and Information Overload: The constant stream of information, including negative news, on social media can contribute to heightened anxiety levels.

6. Highlight Reels vs. Reality: Social media presents curated versions of people's lives—highlighting achievements, vacations, and happy moments. However, this doesn't reflect the full reality. Gen Z may feel pressure to maintain a perfect image, leading to anxiety.

Strategies to Mitigate Social Media's Impact on Anxiety:

1. Set Boundaries: Establish clear boundaries for social media use, such as limiting screen time or creating tech-free zones or times in the day.

2.Practice Mindful Engagement: Encourage mindful engagement with social media by being present and intentional when using these platforms. Encourage Gen Z to be mindful of their social media use. Limit scrolling time, unfollow accounts that trigger negative emotions, and focus on positive content.

3. Curate Your Feed: Follow accounts that promote positivity, creativity, and well-being, and unfollow those that contribute to feelings of anxiety or inadequacy.

4. Practice Self-Awareness: Be aware of your emotions when using social media and take a break if you find yourself feeling anxious or overwhelmed.

5. Seek Support: If anxiety persists, recommend seeking professional support. Therapists can guide coping strategies and provide tools to manage social media-related stress. Reach out to friends, family, or mental health professionals for support if you are struggling with anxiety related to social media use.

Recognizing the link between social media and anxiety, we can work to mitigate its negative impact and promote healthier digital habits that contribute to overall well-being.

Consider this for more Strategies for Managing Social Media-Induced Anxiety

1.Authenticity: Remind them that social media doesn't show the whole picture. Encourage authenticity and vulnerability. Sharing struggles and imperfections can reduce the pressure to appear perfect.

2.Digital Detox: Regular Lu disconnect from social media. Set specific times for checking notifications and avoid screens before bedtime.

3.Positive Communities: Encourage participation in positive online communities. Connecting with like-minded individuals can combat loneliness and anxiety.

Social media can be a powerful tool for connection and self-expression, but it's important to use it mindfully.

2.3. Academic and Career Pressures

Academic and career pressures can significantly contribute to anxiety among Gen Z. As they navigate an increasingly competitive educational and professional landscape, many individuals in this generation face high expectations and mounting stress.

Academic Pressures:

1. High Stakes Testing: Standardised tests, such as college entrance exams, can create intense pressure to perform well and lead to anxiety.

2. Coursework and Grades: Heavy course loads and a focus on maintaining high grades can contribute to feelings of stress and anxiety.

3. Extracurricular Activities: Balancing schoolwork with extracurricular activities can lead to time management challenges and increased anxiety.

4. College Admissions: The competitive nature of college admissions, coupled with the rising cost of higher education, can contribute to anxiety about securing a spot at a desired institution.

Academic Pressure and Mental Health

1. College Students: Research shows that academic pressure is a significant contributor to mental health problems among college students. Nearly half of all participants in a study ranked mental health as the most important issue on campus. The most commonly cited cause. Academic rigor—the pressure of academics. Students often describe this pressure as what "keeps them up at night."

2. External Measures of Success: When discussing academic pressure, students frequently focus on achieving external measures of success. This includes securing a high grade-point average (GPA) or performing well on assignments and exams. The intense emphasis on grades and GPA can lead to stress and anxiety.

Effects of Academic Pressure
1. Depression: Excessive academic pressure can contribute to feelings of depression.

2. Anxiety: The fear of not meeting academic expectations can lead to anxiety.

3. Poor Sleep Quality: Stress from academic demands affects sleep quality.

4. Substance Use: Some students turn to substances as a coping mechanism.

5. High Levels of Stress and Burnout: The constant pressure takes a toll on mental well-being.

6. Depersonalization: Feeling detached from oneself due to stress and pressure.

Career Pressures:

1. Job Market Uncertainty: Rapidly changing industries, technological advancements, and economic fluctuations can create uncertainty and anxiety about career prospects and stability.

2. Income and Financial Security: Concerns about earning a sufficient income, paying off student loans, and achieving financial security can contribute to anxiety about career decisions.

3. Work-Life Balance: Balancing career aspirations with personal life goals can be challenging and lead to anxiety about making trade-offs or sacrifices.

4.Professional Development: The need for continuous learning and skill development in the face of rapid technological change can create pressure and anxiety about remaining competitive in the job market.

Strategies to Manage Academic and Career Pressures:

1. Set Realistic Goals: Establish attainable goals that prioritise your well-being and consider your unique strengths, interests, and values.

2. Seek Support: Reach out to friends, family, mentors, or mental health professionals for guidance and support when facing academic or career challenges.

3. Develop Time Management Skills: Learn effective time management techniques to balance academic or career responsibilities with self-care and leisure activities.

4. Explore Multiple Paths: Recognize that there are multiple paths to success and fulfilment, and be open to exploring different options in education and career development.

5. Practice Self-Compassion: Treat yourself with kindness and understanding during challenging times and acknowledge that setbacks are opportunities for learning and growth.

Addressing academic and career pressures is essential to promoting mental well-being among Gen Z. Your well-being matters. Seek help when needed, and prioritise self-care during your academic journey.

The benefits of understanding and addressing anxiety, especially for Generation Z:

1. Improved Mental Health: By acknowledging anxiety and implementing strategies to manage it, individuals can experience improved mental well-being. This includes reduced stress, better emotional regulation, and enhanced overall happiness.

2.   Enhanced   Resilience: Learning coping mechanisms and resilience strategies equips Gen Z with tools to navigate life's challenges. Resilience allows them to bounce back from setbacks and adapt to changing circumstances.

3. Healthier Relationships: Managing anxiety positively impacts relationships. Effective communication, empathy, and self-awareness contribute to healthier interactions with peers, family, and romantic partners.

4. Academic Success: Reduced anxiety leads to better focus, concentration, and academic performance. Gen Z can excel in their studies when anxiety is managed effectively.

4. Career Advancement: Anxiety management skills are crucial in the workplace. Gen Z can thrive professionally by handling stress, maintaining work-life balance, and building strong professional relationships.

5. Physical Health: Chronic anxiety affects physical health. By addressing anxiety, Gen Z can reduce the risk of stress-related illnesses and promote overall wellness.

Investing in mental health pays dividends across various aspects of life.

2.4. Environmental and Societal Influences

Environmental and societal influences can significantly impact anxiety levels among Gen Z. Growing up in a world faced with numerous challenges, this generation is acutely aware of various issues that affect their lives and future. Some key factors include:

1. Social Factors and Environmental Problems: Environmental sociologists examine how human behaviour, decision-making, and institutions impact the environment. They explore issues like pollution, resource management, and climate change.

i. Climate Change: The increasing threat of climate change, including extreme weather events, rising sea levels, and the loss of biodiversity, can create a sense of existential dread and anxiety about the future.

ii. Pollution: Exposure to pollution, such as air and water contamination, can negatively impact physical health and contribute to mental health issues, including anxiety.

iii. Urbanisation: Rapid urbanisation can lead to overcrowding, increased noise, and reduced green spaces, potentially exacerbating anxiety and stress.

2. Social Construction of Environmental Problems: Environmental sociologists examine how human behavior, decision-making, and institutions impact the environment. They explore issues like pollution, resource management, and climate change.

i. Political Instability: Growing up amidst political polarisation, global conflicts, and social unrest can contribute to anxiety about safety, security, and the future of society.

ii. Economic Inequality: Widening income gaps and limited social mobility can create financial anxiety and concerns about future economic stability.

iii. Discrimination and Injustice: Experiences with discrimination, racism, and social injustice can cause anxiety and negatively impact mental health, particularly for marginalized groups.

3. Holistic Perspective: Environmental sociology emerged in response to the environmental movement of the 1960s. It integrates physical context (our environment) with social factors. Think of it as sociology with an eco-conscious twist.

Strategies to Address Environmental and Societal Influences on Anxiety:

1. Climate Action: Encouraging climate action at individual, community, and governmental levels can help alleviate anxiety related to climate change by promoting a sense of agency and hope for the future.

2. Environmental Conservation: Supporting local conservation efforts and engaging in sustainable practices can contribute to a healthier environment, positively impacting mental well-being.

3. Social Advocacy: Engaging in social advocacy and activism can empower individuals to address issues related to inequality, discrimination, and injustice, promoting a more inclusive and equitable society.

4. Community Engagement: Building connections within local communities can help foster a sense of belonging, support, and collective resilience in the face of environmental and societal challenges.

5. Mental Health Support: Providing access to mental health resources, such as therapy and support groups, can help individuals cope with anxiety stemming from environmental and societal influences.

Key Concepts in Environmental Sociology

1. Carrying Capacity: This refers to the maximum amount of life that an area can sustain given its limited natural resources. When the commons (shared resources like air, water, and ecosystems) are threatened, the environment's carrying capacity is degraded.

2. The Commons: These are collective resources shared by humans—natural elements beyond private ownership or commodification. Protecting the commons is important for sustaining life and maintaining ecological balance.

3. Existential Dualism: Humans co-evolve with other species, sharing ecological dependencies. Simultaneously, our cultural uniqueness, innovation, and institutions set us apart. Balancing these aspects is important .

Environmental sociology helps us understand, address, and solve environmental challenges. It's a vital field for creating a sustainable future.

Chapter 3

3.0 Root Causes of Anxiety

Anxiety is a complex mental health condition that can stem from various root causes. Identifying and understanding these underlying factors can help in developing targeted strategies to manage and treat anxiety effectively.

Causes

1. Genetics: Anxiety can run in families, indicating a genetic component to the disorder. Individuals with a family history of anxiety are more likely to develop anxiety themselves.

2. Biology: Imbalances in neurotransmitters, such as serotonin and dopamine, can contribute to anxiety. Additionally, certain medical conditions or medications may cause or exacerbate anxiety symptoms.

3. Learned Behaviours: Growing up in an environment where anxiety is modelled or reinforced can lead to the development of anxious behaviours and thought patterns. This is often seen in individuals who have experienced trauma or abuse during childhood.

4. Life Experiences: Traumatic events, chronic stress, or significant life changes can trigger anxiety. These experiences can range from accidents and natural disasters to personal losses and relationship difficulties.

5. **Cognitive Distortions:** Unrealistic or unhelpful thinking patterns, such as catastrophizing, all-or-nothing thinking, and overgeneralization, can contribute to anxiety by fostering a negative perception of oneself, others, or the world.

6. Societal Factors: As discussed earlier, environmental and societal influences, such as climate change, discrimination, and economic instability, can contribute to the development of anxiety in individuals.

7. Substance Abuse: Substance abuse, such as excessive alcohol consumption or drug use, can lead to increased anxiety. Additionally, withdrawal from certain substances can also trigger anxiety symptoms.

Strategies to Address Root Causes of Anxiety:

1. Medication: For some individuals, medications such as selective serotonin reuptake inhibitors (SSRIs) and benzodiazepines may be prescribed to address biological causes of anxiety.

2. Therapy: Various forms of therapy, such as cognitive-behavioural therapy (CBT), can help individuals identify and challenge cognitive distortions and learned behaviours contributing to anxiety.

3. Mindfulness Practices: Mindfulness and meditation practices can help individuals manage anxiety by promoting present-moment awareness and non-judgmental acceptance of thoughts and feelings.

4. Exercise and Nutrition: Regular exercise, a balanced diet, and adequate sleep can contribute to improved mental well-being and reduced anxiety.

5. Support Networks: Building and maintaining supportive relationships with friends, family, or support groups can help individuals cope with anxiety and navigate life challenges.

Understanding and addressing the root causes of anxiety is crucial in developing effective strategies to manage this mental health condition.

Consider this for more causes of anxiety, especially in the context of Generation Z:

1. Social Pressures and Expectations: Gen Z faces immense pressure to conform to societal norms, achieve academic success, and maintain an ideal online presence. These expectations can lead to anxiety about fitting in, meeting standards, and being accepted.

2. Technological Overload: The digital age exposes Gen Z to constant stimuli—social media, notifications, and information overload. This hyperconnectivity can overwhelm their mental well-being, contributing to anxiety.

3. Economic Uncertainty: Gen Z grew up during economic recessions, witnessing job instability and student loan debt. Financial worries impact mental health, leading to anxiety about the future.

4. Climate Anxiety: Environmental concerns, climate change, and the urgency to address ecological issues weigh heavily on Gen Z. Fear for the planet's future can cause anxiety.

5. Academic Stress: The pressure to excel academically, secure scholarships, and compete in a globalised world can lead to anxiety. Balancing coursework, extracurriculars, and personal life is challenging.

6. Social Isolation: Despite digital connectivity, Gen Z experiences loneliness. Isolation, lack of meaningful connections, and fear of missing out contribute to anxiety.

7. Health and Well-being: Concerns about physical health, body image, and wellness impact mental health. Gen Z grapples with self-care, nutrition, and exercise-related anxiety.

3.1. Biological and Psychological Factors

Biological and psychological factors play significant roles in the development and persistence of anxiety. Understanding these factors is important in addressing anxiety effectively and improving mental health outcomes.

Biological Factors:

1. Genetics: As mentioned earlier, anxiety can run in families, suggesting a genetic component. Research indicates that individuals with a parent or sibling with anxiety are more likely to develop the disorder themselves.

2. Neurotransmitters: Imbalances in neurotransmitters, such as serotonin, dopamine, and norepinephrine, can contribute to anxiety. These neurotransmitters are responsible for regulating mood, emotions, and the stress response.

3. Hormones: Hormonal imbalances, such as those related to thyroid function or cortisol levels, can also play a role in anxiety.

4. Brain Structure and Function: Research suggests that abnormalities in specific brain regions, such as the amygdala and hippocampus, may contribute to anxiety. These areas are involved in processing emotions and memories, particularly those related to fear and stress.

Psychological Factors:

1. Learned Behaviours: Individuals who grow up in an environment where anxiety is modelled or reinforced may develop anxious behaviours and thought patterns. This can be especially prevalent in those who have experienced trauma or abuse during childhood.

2. Cognitive Distortions: Unrealistic or unhelpful thinking patterns, such as catastrophizing, all-or-nothing thinking, and overgeneralization, can contribute to anxiety by fostering a negative perception of oneself, others, or the world.

3. Emotional Regulation: Difficulties in managing emotions effectively can lead to increased anxiety. This may involve suppressing or avoiding emotions, which can exacerbate anxiety in the long run.

4. Stress and Coping Skills: Inadequate coping skills or prolonged exposure to stress can contribute to the development of anxiety. This may include difficulties in problem-solving, assertiveness, or seeking social support.

Strategies to Address Biological and Psychological Factors

1. Medication: For some individuals, medications such as selective serotonin reuptake inhibitors (SSRIs) and benzodiazepines may be prescribed to address biological causes of anxiety.

2. Therapy: Various forms of therapy, such as cognitive-behavioural therapy (CBT), can help individuals identify and challenge cognitive distortions and learned behaviours contributing to anxiety.

3. **Mindfulness Practices:** Mindfulness and meditation practices can help individuals manage anxiety by promoting present-moment awareness and non-judgmental acceptance of thoughts and feelings.

4. **Stress Management Techniques:**Developing healthy stress management techniques, such as relaxation exercises, time management skills, and assertiveness training, can help individuals cope with anxiety-inducing situations.

5. **Lifestyle Changes:** Incorporating regular exercise, a balanced diet, and adequate sleep can contribute to improved mental well-being and reduced anxiety.

Anxiety is multifaceted, and addressing both biological and psychological factors is important for effective management.

3.2. Family Dynamics and Peer Relationships

Family dynamics and peer relationships can significantly impact anxiety levels among individuals, particularly during childhood and adolescence. Understanding these influences can help in addressing anxiety and promoting mental health.

Family Dynamics:

1. Parenting Style: Parenting styles that are overprotective, overly critical, or neglectful can contribute to anxiety in children. These parenting behaviours may prevent children from developing healthy coping skills and self-esteem.

2. Family Conflict: Exposure to frequent arguments or conflicts within the family can create an environment of stress and anxiety.

3. Modelling of Anxiety: Children may learn anxious behaviours and thought patterns from parents or caregivers who display anxiety themselves.

4. Trauma or Abuse: Experiencing trauma or abuse within the family can have long-lasting effects on mental health, including increased anxiety.

Peer Relationships:

1. Social Acceptance: Children and adolescents may experience anxiety related to social acceptance, including the fear of being rejected or bullied by peers.

2. Friendship Quality: Having supportive and positive friendships can serve as a protective factor against anxiety, while toxic or unstable friendships may contribute to increased anxiety.

3. Peer Pressure: Pressure from peers to engage in risky or uncomfortable behaviours can lead to anxiety and stress.

Strategies to Address Family Dynamics and Peer Relationships:

1. Family Therapy: Family therapy can help address conflicts, improve communication, and promote healthier family dynamics.

2. Social Skills Training: Social skills training can help individuals develop the skills necessary for building and maintaining positive relationships with peers.

3. Parenting Workshops: Parenting workshops can provide parents with the knowledge and skills to support their children's emotional well-being and manage anxiety effectively.

4. Support Groups: Joining support groups can provide individuals with a sense of belonging and help them learn from others who have experienced similar challenges.

Healthy family dynamics and supportive peer relationships contribute to resilience and overall mental health.

3.3. Economic Uncertainty and Future Prospects

Economic uncertainty plays a significant role in shaping the future prospects of individuals and communities. The state of the economy can influence various aspects of life, including job security, financial stability, and access to resources.

Effects of Economic Uncertainty on Future Prospects

1. Employment: During periods of economic uncertainty, job markets can become unstable, leading to layoffs, underemployment, and reduced job opportunities. This can make it challenging for individuals to secure stable and well-paying jobs, affecting their financial security and career growth.

2. Income and Savings: Economic uncertainty can result in stagnant or declining wages, making it difficult for individuals to save money and accumulate wealth. This can hinder long-term financial planning, such as purchasing a home, investing in education, or saving for retirement.

3. Access to Resources: Reduced financial stability can limit access to essential resources, such as healthcare, education, and housing. This can have long-term consequences for individuals and communities, perpetuating inequalities, and affecting overall well-being.

4. Mental Health: Economic uncertainty can exacerbate stress and anxiety, as individuals worry about their financial situations and future prospects.

Strategies for Navigating Economic Uncertainty

1. Diversifying Income Streams: Developing multiple sources of income can provide a safety net during uncertain economic times. This could involve pursuing part-time jobs, freelancing, or starting a small business.

2. Building Emergency Savings: Creating a financial cushion by setting aside money in an emergency fund can help individuals weather periods of economic uncertainty.

3. Seeking Professional Guidance: Consulting with financial advisors or career counsellors can provide valuable insights and guidance for navigating economic challenges and improving future prospects.

4. Continuous Learning and Skill Development: Investing in ongoing education and skill-building can enhance employability and adaptability in a changing job market.

5. Embracing Financial Literacy: Understanding personal finances, budgeting, and investing can empower individuals to make informed decisions and manage their financial resources effectively during periods of economic uncertainty.

Implementing these strategies and fostering a proactive approach to financial management, individuals can better navigate economic uncertainty and improve their future prospects. Additionally, policies that promote economic stability, job creation, and access to resources can play a crucial role in supporting individuals and communities during challenging economic times.

3.4. The Impact of Global Issues

Global issues significantly impact the economy and, consequently, individual and community prospects. These issues are diverse and interconnected, ranging from geopolitical tensions and climate change to technological disruptions and public health crises.

Major Global Issues Affecting the Economy and Future Prospects

1. Geopolitical Tensions: Conflicts and political instability can disrupt trade, impact financial markets, and create uncertainties for businesses and investors, affecting global economic growth.

2. Climate Change: The increasing frequency and severity of climate-related events, such as natural disasters, can damage infrastructure, disrupt supply chains, and negatively impact industries like agriculture, insurance, and tourism.

3. Technological Disruptions: Rapid advancements in technology can create new industries and opportunities but can also lead to job displacement, income inequality, and privacy concerns.

4. Public Health Crises: Pandemics and other health crises can overwhelm healthcare systems, disrupt economic activity, and strain public resources, as seen with the COVID-19 pandemic.

Strategies to Mitigate the Impact of Global Issues:

1. Investing in Resilience: Governments, businesses, and communities can invest in infrastructure, technology, and human capital to enhance resilience to global shocks and disruptions.

2. Fostering International Collaboration: Countries can work together to address global challenges through diplomacy, trade agreements, and shared commitments to sustainable development.

3. Adapting to Technological Change: Promoting digital literacy, investing in education and job training, and fostering innovation can help individuals and economies adapt to and benefit from technological disruptions.

4. Strengthening Public Health Systems: Improving global health surveillance, investing in healthcare infrastructure, and ensuring equitable access to healthcare services can help mitigate the impact of public health crises.

Individual Strategies:

1. Diversifying Income Streams: Developing multiple sources of income and investing in assets that can withstand global shocks can provide financial stability during uncertain times.

2. Continuous Learning and Skill Development: Updating skills and knowledge can enhance employability and adaptability to changing economic landscapes.

3. Sustainable Practices: Adopting sustainable practices, such as conserving energy, reducing waste, and supporting environmentally-friendly products, can contribute to a greener and more resilient future.

Chapter 4

4.0 Building Resilience

Building resilience involves developing the ability to navigate and adapt to life's challenges, stresses, and adversity while maintaining a relatively stable and healthy mental well-being.

Building Resilience:

1. Understanding Resilience Definition: Resilience is the ability to bounce back from adversity, setbacks, and stress. It's not about avoiding challenges but rather adapting and growing stronger through them. **Metaphor:** Think of resilience as a tree that bends during a storm but doesn't break. It draws nourishment from its roots and adapts to changing conditions.

2. Components of Resilience Emotional Regulation: Resilient individuals manage their emotions effectively. They recognize feelings, express them constructively, and avoid emotional overwhelm. **Cognitive Flexibility:** Being open-minded and adaptable helps navigate unexpected situations.

Resilient people adjust their thinking patterns and find alternative solutions.

Social Support: Strong relationships act as buffers against stress. Cultivating a support network of friends, family, and mentors enhances resilience.

Self-Compassion: Treating oneself kindly during tough times fosters resilience. Acknowledge imperfections without self-criticism. Sense of **Purpose:** Having a clear purpose or meaningful goals provides motivation and resilience. It's the "why" behind our actions.

Practical Strategies for Resilience

1. Mindfulness and Grounding Techniques: Practise mindfulness meditation to stay present and reduce anxiety. Ground yourself by noticing sensory details (sight, sound, touch) during stressful moments.

2. Learn from Adversity: View challenges as opportunities for growth.

3. Learn from Past Experiences: Reflect on previous challenges and the strategies used to overcome them, and apply those lessons to future situations.

4. Ask: "What can I learn from this?" Reframe setbacks as stepping stones toward resilience.

5. Develop Coping Skills: Identify healthy coping mechanisms (e.g., exercise, journaling, creative outlets). Avoid maladaptive coping (e.g., substance abuse, avoidance).

6. Engage in Regular Physical Activity: Exercise can help reduce stress, improve mood, and promote mental resilience.

7. Build Social Connections: Surrounding yourself with supportive individuals can provide comfort, encouragement, and practical help during challenging times. Invest time in nurturing relationships. Reach out to friends or family during tough times.

8. Set Realistic Goals: Break down big goals into smaller, achievable steps. Celebrate progress along the way.

Bonus Topic:
Post-Traumatic Growth Definition: Post-traumatic growth (PTG) refers to positive changes that occur after adversity.
Factors: PTG often emerges from trauma, loss, or major life events.

Areas of Growth: Personal strength, appreciation of life, improved relationships, spiritual growth, and new possibilities.

4.1. What is Resilience

Resilience is the ability to navigate and adapt to life's challenges, stresses, and adversity while maintaining a relatively stable and healthy mental well-being. When faced with adversity—such as trauma, illness, workplace issues, or relationship struggles—resilient individuals can "bounce back." They demonstrate mental, emotional, and behavioral flexibility, adapting well to difficult experiences. Rather than avoiding or denying difficulties, resilient people face them head-on, using healthy coping skills and available resources to manage the situation. Resilience doesn't mean experiencing less distress; instead, it fosters strength and growth, often leaving individuals stronger than before.

Key aspects of resilience include:

1. Self-Care and Stress Management:

Self-care and stress management are important aspects of maintaining overall health and well-being. prioritizing self-care and implementing effective stress management techniques, individuals can better navigate life's challenges and foster personal growth.

i. Physical Well-Being: Prioritizing sleep, nutrition, and exercise is crucial. Adequate rest and nourishment support mental resilience. When we're physically well, we can better handle stressors.

ii. Stress Reduction Techniques: Consider mindfulness practices, progressive muscle relaxation, or yoga. These techniques help manage stress by grounding us in the present moment and calming the nervous system.

2. Learned Optimism and Positive Thinking:

Learned optimism and positive thinking are powerful tools that can help individuals develop resilience and improve their overall well-being. By consciously cultivating optimistic thought patterns and engaging in positive thinking practices, people can overcome challenges more effectively and foster personal growth.

i. Optimistic Explanatory Style: This concept, popularized by psychologist Martin Seligman, emphasizes how we explain events to ourselves. Resilient individuals tend to attribute setbacks to external, temporary factors (e.g., "I didn't get the job because they needed someone with a different skill set") rather than internal, permanent ones (e.g., "I'm not good enough for any job"). Optimism fosters resilience.

ii. Gratitude Practice: Regularly expressing gratitude—whether through journaling, verbal affirmations, or acts of kindness—enhances our overall well-being. It shifts our focus from what's lacking to what we appreciate.

3. Adaptability and Flexibility:

Adaptability and flexibility are crucial skills that enable individuals to effectively respond to changes and uncertainty in their environment. Developing these qualities allows people to embrace new experiences, learn from challenges, and cultivate resilience.

i. Acceptance of Change: Resilience involves accepting that change is inevitable. Rather than resisting it, we learn to adapt. Think of change as an opportunity for growth, even when it feels uncomfortable.

ii. Problem-Solving Skills: Resilient individuals break down challenges into manageable steps. They approach problems with a solution-oriented mindset. Effective problem-solving builds confidence and resilience.

4. Resilience in Creativity and Innovation:

Resilience in creativity and innovation refers to the ability to persist and adapt through the challenges and uncertainties inherent in the creative process. Developing this resilience, individuals and teams can foster a creative and innovative mindset that enables them to overcome obstacles and generate novel ideas.

i. Creative Problem-Solving: Resilience fuels creativity. When faced with obstacles, our brains engage in lateral thinking. We explore unconventional solutions and find new paths.

ii. Embracing Failure: Resilient creators view failure as part of the process. Each setback provides valuable feedback. learning, adapting, and iterating, they eventually succeed.

5. Cultivating Emotional Intelligence:

Emotional Intelligence is the ability to understand, manage, and express emotions effectively. It involves developing self-awareness, empathy, and the skills to navigate interpersonal relationships successfully.

i. Self-Awareness: Understand your emotions, triggers, and patterns. Self-awareness empowers better decision-making and helps us navigate challenges more effectively.

ii. Empathy: Connect with others by understanding their emotions.

6. Building a Resilient Community:

Constructing a robust and adaptable community involves establishing a supportive and inclusive environment where individuals can thrive, even in the face of adversity. A resilient community fosters strong social bonds, encourages open communication, and collaborates to address challenges.

i. Collective Resilience: Communities that support each other thrive. Whether it's a close-knit group of friends, a workplace team, or an online community, fostering connections and offering mutual support enhances resilience.

ii. Shared Values: Communities with shared values provide a sense of belonging and purpose. When we align with others who share our principles, we feel more resilient and motivated.

Resilience is not a fixed trait but rather a set of skills and attributes that can be cultivated and strengthened over time through various strategies and practices. Building resilience enables individuals to face life's challenges with greater ease, promoting personal growth and well-being.

4.2. The Science Behind Resilience

Resilience is the process of successfully adapting to challenging life experiences, adversity, or significant sources of stress. Research in psychology, neuroscience, and related fields has explored the mechanisms underlying resilience and identified factors that contribute to an individual's capacity to bounce back from difficult situations.

1. The Role of Neuroplasticity

Neuroplasticity is the brain's remarkable ability to change, adapt, and reorganize itself in response to various experiences and environmental stimuli throughout an individual's life. It plays a important role in shaping resilience, as it allows for the formation of new neural connections and the strengthening or weakening of existing ones. It allows for the creation of new neural pathways and the modification of existing ones. This process plays a important role in building resilience, as individuals learn from past experiences and develop coping mechanisms to handle future challenges more effectively.

2. The Stress Response System

The body's stress response system is essential in managing challenging situations. This system releases hormones, such as cortisol and adrenaline, to help individuals cope with stressors. Research has shown that resilient individuals often exhibit a more efficient stress response, which allows them to manage stressors and recover more quickly.

3. The Influence of Genetics and Environment

Both genetic and environmental factors play a role in shaping resilience. While certain genes may predispose individuals to be more or less resilient, early life experiences, social support, and coping strategies also influence resilience. Research suggests that a positive environment and strong social connections can buffer the effects of adverse experiences, thereby promoting resilience.

The Importance of Emotional Regulation and Coping Strategies

Individuals with strong emotional regulation skills and effective coping strategies tend to be more resilient. Emotional regulation involves identifying and managing emotions in a healthy way, while coping strategies are actions taken to reduce the impact of stressors. Examples of adaptive coping strategies include seeking social support, engaging in physical activity, and practicing relaxation techniques.

Building Resilience Through Interventions

Research has shown that resilience can be cultivated through targeted interventions, such as cognitive-behavioral therapy (CBT), mindfulness-based stress reduction (MBSR), and resilience training programs. These interventions aim to improve emotional regulation, coping strategies, and overall well-being, thereby enhancing individuals' resilience.

key insights

1. Supportive Relationships: Resilience thrives when children have stable, committed relationships with supportive adults. These relationships provide a crucial foundation for healthy development.
Regular interactions ("serve and return") between caregivers and children scaffold essential capacities, such as planning, behavior regulation, and adaptability.

2. Brain and Stress Response: The developing brain relies on these interactions. In their absence, optimal brain architecture doesn't form.

Toxic stress, caused by prolonged adversity without supportive relationships, affects overall health and mental well-being.

3. Characteristics of Resilience: Resilience involves both internal disposition and external experiences.

Measurable responses occur in kids' brains, immune systems, and genes during stress.

Certain characteristics predispose children to positive outcomes despite adversity.

The science behind resilience highlights the importance of neuroplasticity, the stress response system, genetics and environment, emotional regulation, and coping strategies in promoting an individual's capacity to adapt to adversity. Understanding these factors, researchers can develop interventions to help individuals cultivate resilience and lead more fulfilling lives.

4.3. Developing a Resilient Mindset

Developing a resilient mindset involves cultivating attitudes, beliefs, and behaviors that promote adaptability and help individuals navigate life's challenges effectively. A resilient mindset fosters personal growth and well-being, enabling individuals to bounce back from adversity and thrive in the face of stress and uncertainty.

Key Components of a Resilient Mindset:

1. Growth Mindset: Embracing a growth mindset involves believing that abilities and intelligence can be developed through dedication, effort, and learning from challenges. This mindset fosters resilience by encouraging individuals to view setbacks as opportunities for growth and improvement.

2. Positive Attributions: Adopting a positive attribution style involves interpreting challenges and setbacks in a constructive manner. Resilient individuals focus on temporary factors, personal growth, and situational causes, rather than dwelling on negative aspects or personal shortcomings.

3. Self-Efficacy: Developing a strong sense of self-efficacy entails believing in one's ability to successfully navigate and overcome challenges. This belief fosters resilience by enhancing motivation and perseverance in the face of adversity.

4. Emotional Regulation: Effective emotional regulation is essential for a resilient mindset. This involves recognizing, understanding, and managing one's emotions in a healthy way, which can mitigate the negative impact of stressors on well-being.

5. **Flexibility:** Cultivating mental flexibility enables individuals to adapt to changing circumstances and unexpected challenges. This includes being open to new ideas, approaches, and perspectives, as well as modifying plans and expectations as needed.

Effective strategies to build mental toughness and resilience

1. Learn from Past Bounce-Backs: Reflect on difficult times you've overcome. Journaling about past experiences helps you draw strength from adversity. The past provides rich territory for learning and growth.

2. Don't Listen to 2 AM Voices: Late-night worries often magnify problems. Challenge negative thoughts and avoid catastrophizing. Remind yourself that emotions at 2 AM aren't always rational.

3. Stop Worrying: Focus on what you can control. Worrying about the uncontrollable drains mental energy.

4. Rethink Goal Setting: Set realistic, adaptive goals. Be flexible and adjust as needed. Embrace progress over perfection.

5. Deal with Imposter Syndrome: Recognize imposter feelings as common. Many successful people experience self-doubt. Celebrate your achievements and acknowledge your competence.

6. Watch Out for Catastrophic Thinking: Avoid spiraling into worst-case scenarios. Challenge irrational thoughts. Replace catastrophic thinking with balanced, realistic perspectives.

Resilience is a skill that can be honed through practice and discipline. By adopting these techniques, you'll build mental strength and face life's challenges with confidence.

Consider this for More Strategies for Developing a Resilient Mindset:

1. **Reframe Challenges:** View obstacles as opportunities for growth and learning, rather than as roadblocks.

2. **Set Realistic Goals:** Establish attainable objectives that provide a sense of purpose and direction, while allowing for flexibility in the face of challenges.

3. **Foster Positive Relationships:** Surround oneself with supportive individuals who encourage personal growth and provide assistance during difficult times.

4. **Practice Mindfulness:** Engage in mindfulness exercises to increase self-awareness, promote acceptance, and enhance emotional regulation.

5. **Develop Problem-Solving Skills:** Enhance the ability to analyse situations objectively, brainstorm solutions, and implement effective strategies to overcome challenges.

4.4. Overcoming Setbacks and Challenges

Overcoming setbacks and challenges is important aspect of personal growth and resilience. It involves developing strategies and skills to manage adversity effectively, learn from experiences, and maintain a positive outlook in the face of obstacles.

effective strategies to navigate these difficult moments:

1. Embrace a Growth Mindset: View challenges as opportunities for learning and personal growth, rather than as insurmountable obstacles.

2. Set Realistic Goals: Establish specific, achievable objectives to maintain focus and motivation during difficult times.

3. Develop Problem-Solving Skills: Enhance the ability to analyse situations, generate potential solutions, and implement effective strategies.

4. **Build Support Networks:** Cultivate relationships with supportive individuals who provide encouragement, advice, and assistance in overcoming challenges.

5. **Practice Emotional Regulation:** Develop the capacity to recognize, understand, and manage emotions in a healthy way to mitigate the impact of stressors on well-being.

6. **Foster Resilience:** Engage in activities that promote resilience, such as mindfulness, physical exercise, and maintaining a balanced lifestyle.

Learning from Setbacks and Challenges:

1. **Reflect on Experiences:** Analyse past challenges to identify areas for improvement and personal growth.

2. **Seek Feedback:** Solicit constructive input from others to gain valuable insights and perspectives on overcoming obstacles.

3. **Develop Self-Awareness:** Increase understanding of personal strengths, weaknesses, and emotional triggers to better navigate future challenges.

4. Embrace Failure as a Learning Opportunity: Recognize that setbacks provide valuable lessons and contribute to personal growth and resilience.

Maintaining a Positive Outlook:

1. Practice Gratitude: Focus on positive aspects of life and express appreciation for personal accomplishments and support from others.

2. Visualise Success: Envision overcoming challenges and achieving goals to boost motivation and self-confidence.

3. Encourage Optimism: Adopt a hopeful, optimistic mindset that focuses on opportunities for grerowth and positive outcomes.

Chapter 5

5.0 Mental Health Strategies

Taking care of one's mental health is crucial for overall well-being and resilience. Implementing effective mental health strategies can help individuals manage stress, navigate challenges, and maintain a positive outlook on life.

Mental Health Strategies for Well-being:

1. Practice Mindfulness: Engage in mindfulness exercises, such as meditation, yoga, or deep breathing, to increase self-awareness, reduce stress, and improve emotional regulation.

2. Establish a Routine: Create a structured daily schedule to provide stability, consistency, and a sense of accomplishment.

3. Set Boundaries: Establish healthy limits in personal and professional relationships to maintain emotional balance and prevent burnout.

4. Cultivate Hobbies and Interests: Dedicate time to activities that bring joy and fulfilment, promoting relaxation and enhancing overall well-being.

5. Seek Professional Support: Consult with mental health professionals, such as therapists or counselors, for guidance and assistance in managing mental health concerns.

Strategies for Building Emotional Resilience:

1. Practice Gratitude: Focus on positive aspects of life and express appreciation for personal accomplishments and support from others.

2. Reframe Challenges: View obstacles as opportunities for growth and learning, rather than as insurmountable roadblocks.

3. Develop Problem-Solving Skills: Enhance the ability to analyze situations, generate potential solutions, and implement effective strategies.

4. Practice Self-Care: Prioritize personal needs and engage in activities that promote physical, emotional, and mental well-being.

Strategies for Maintaining a Positive Outlook:

1. Encourage Optimism: Adopt a hopeful, optimistic mindset that focuses on opportunities for growth and positive outcomes.

2. Celebrate Success: Recognize and celebrate personal achievements, no matter how small, to boost self-esteem and motivation.

3. Limit Exposure to Negativity: Minimize time spent consuming negative media or engaging in negative self-talk, focusing instead on positive influences and affirmations.

4. Set Realistic Goals: Establish specific, achievable objectives to maintain focus and motivation during difficult times.

incorporating these mental health strategies into daily life, individuals can promote overall well-being, build emotional resilience, and maintain a positive outlook. Proactively managing mental health contributes to personal growth, healthier relationships, and greater success in navigating life's challenges.

5.1. Effective Stress Management Techniques

Effectively managing stress is vital for preserving mental, emotional, and physical well-being.

Implementing practical stress management techniques can help individuals cope with life's challenges, reduce anxiety, and enhance overall resilience.

Techniques for Managing Stress:

1. Mindfulness and Meditation Practice: Engage in mindfulness exercises or meditation to increase self-awareness, reduce anxiety, and improve emotional regulation.

2. Regular Exercise: Participate in physical activities, such as walking, running, or yoga, to release tension, improve mood, and promote relaxation.

3. Healthy Diet: Maintain a balanced diet, rich in fruits, vegetables, and lean proteins, to provide the body with essential nutrients and support stress management.

4. Adequate Sleep: Prioritise getting 7-9 hours of quality sleep each night to rejuvenate the body and mind, enabling better stress management.

5. Time Management: Plan daily tasks, set priorities, and delegate responsibilities when possible to maintain a balanced workload and reduce stress.

Strategies for Reducing Anxiety:

1. Challenging Negative Thoughts: Identify and challenge negative or unhelpful thought patterns, replacing them with more realistic, positive alternatives.

2. Deep Breathing Exercises: Engage in deep breathing techniques to reduce anxiety, slow heart rate, and promote relaxation.

5. Calming Environment: Design a relaxing personal space with calming colors, soothing sounds, and comfortable furnishings to alleviate anxiety and encourage relaxation.

6. Seeking Support: Share concerns with trusted friends, family members, or mental health professionals to gain valuable insights, advice, and encouragement.

7. Progressive Muscle Relaxation: Practice systematically tensing and releasing muscle groups to reduce physical tension and anxiety.

Techniques for Enhancing Resilience:

1. Realistic Goal Setting: Establish specific, achievable objectives to maintain focus and motivation during challenging times.

2. Fostering Positive Relationships: Cultivate supportive relationships with friends, family, or colleagues who provide encouragement and assistance.

3. Self-Care Practice: Engage in activities that promote physical, emotional, and mental well-being, such as hobbies, exercise, or personal interests.

4. Problem-Solving Skills Development: Enhance the ability to analyze situations, generate potential solutions, and implement effective strategies.

utilizing these stress management techniques, individuals can effectively cope with life's challenges, reduce anxiety, and enhance overall resilience. Actively managing stress contributes to improved mental and physical health, increased productivity, and greater satisfaction in daily life.

5.2. Mindfulness and Meditation Practices

Mindfulness and meditation practices are powerful tools for promoting mental and emotional well-being, reducing stress, and increasing self-awareness. These practices involve focusing on the present moment and adopting a non-judgmental attitude towards thoughts, feelings, and sensations. Here are some key mindfulness and meditation techniques:

1. Mindfulness-Based Stress Reduction (MBSR): Developed by Jon Kabat-Zinn, MBSR involves practising various mindfulness techniques, such as body scans, mindful breathing, and mindful movement, to cultivate greater awareness and reduce stress.

2. Vipassana Meditation: Vipassana is an ancient meditation technique that encourages observing and accepting thoughts and emotions without judgment. It helps practitioners gain insight into the impermanent nature of their experiences and reduce suffering.

3. Loving-Kindness Meditation (Metta Bhavana): This practice involves cultivating feelings of warmth, kindness, and compassion towards oneself and others through guided visualisation and the repetition of specific phrases or mantras.

4. Transcendental Meditation (TM): TM involves repeating a specific mantra to help the mind settle down and experience a state of relaxed awareness. This practice aims to reduce stress, improve focus, and promote overall well-being.

5. Guided Visualisation: Guided visualisation involves using mental imagery and sensory experiences to create a relaxed and focused state of mind. This technique can help reduce anxiety, manage stress, and improve sleep quality.

6. Mindful Walking: Mindful walking is the practice of bringing awareness to the physical sensations of walking, such as the pressure of the feet on the ground and the movement of the body. This practice can be done indoors or outdoors and helps cultivate present-moment awareness.

7. Breathing Meditations: Various breathing meditation techniques, such as diaphragmatic breathing or alternate nostril breathing, involve focusing on the breath to calm the mind and reduce stress.

Incorporating mindfulness and meditation practices into daily life, individuals can develop greater self-awareness, manage stress effectively, and enhance their overall well-being. These practices can be adapted to suit individual preferences and needs and can be integrated into various aspects of daily life to cultivate a more mindful and balanced lifestyle.

5.3. Cognitive Behavioral Approaches

Cognitive behavioural approaches are a group of psychotherapeutic techniques that focus on identifying and modifying unhelpful thought patterns, emotions, and behaviours to improve emotional well-being and overall functioning.

Key Cognitive Behavioral Approaches:

1. Cognitive Behavioral Therapy (CBT): CBT is a short-term, goal-oriented therapy that emphasises the role of thoughts and beliefs in shaping emotions and behaviours. CBT aims to help individuals identify and challenge negative or distorted thinking patterns, develop more adaptive thoughts and behaviours, and improve emotional regulation.

2. Dialectical Behavior Therapy (DBT): DBT is an evidence-based therapy initially developed to treat borderline personality disorder but has since been adapted for various mental health issues. DBT focuses on developing mindfulness, interpersonal effectiveness, emotion regulation, and distress tolerance skills to enhance overall functioning and well-being.

3. Rational Emotive Behavior Therapy (REBT): REBT is a form of CBT that emphasizes the role of irrational beliefs in creating emotional distress. This approach aims to help individuals identify, challenge, and replace irrational beliefs with more rational and adaptive thoughts.

4. Acceptance and Commitment Therapy (ACT): ACT encourages individuals to accept and embrace negative thoughts and emotions rather than trying to eliminate them. This approach focuses on developing mindfulness, acceptance, and behavioral change strategies to enhance psychological flexibility and align behaviors with personal values.

Core Principles of Cognitive Behavioral Approaches:

1. Collaborative Therapeutic Relationship: A strong therapeutic alliance between the client and therapist is crucial in cognitive behavioural approaches, as both parties work together to identify and modify unhelpful patterns.

2. Present-Centred Focus: Cognitive behavioural approaches concentrate on current thoughts, emotions, and behaviours, rather than delving extensively into past experiences or unconscious processes.

3. Structured and Goal-Oriented: Treatment plans are typically structured, time-limited, and goal-oriented, with a focus on measurable outcomes.

4. Active and Directive: Therapists play an active role in guiding clients through the therapeutic process, teaching specific skills and strategies, and assigning homework tasks to reinforce learning and practice.

Cognitive behavioural approaches have been proven effective in treating a wide range of mental health issues, including anxiety disorders, depression, eating disorders, and substance use disorders.

5.4. Seeking Professional Help

Seeking professional help for mental health concerns is an essential step in managing and overcoming personal challenges. Professional support can provide valuable guidance, skills, and resources for navigating mental health issues and promoting well-being.

Signs that Professional Help may be Needed:

1. Persistent negative emotions or mood changes, such as sadness, anxiety, or anger.
2. Difficulty coping with daily activities or routine tasks.
3. Changes in appetite, energy levels, or sleep patterns.
4. Feeling overwhelmed, hopeless, or helpless.
5. Increased use of substances, such as alcohol, drugs, or food, to cope with emotions.
6. Difficulty maintaining healthy relationships or problems in work or school.
7. Recurring physical symptoms, such as headaches or stomach issues, with no identifiable medical cause.

Options for Professional Support:

1. Mental Health Professionals: Psychologists, psychiatrists, therapists, and counselors offer a range of evidence-based treatments and support services for individuals with mental health concerns.

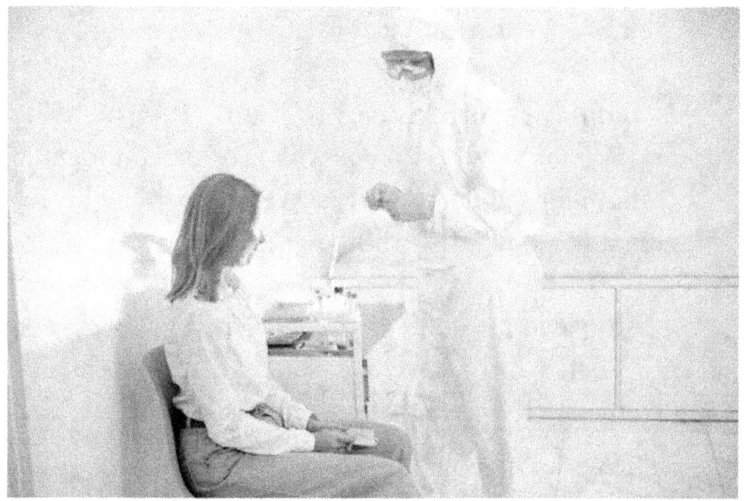

2. **Support Groups:** Participating in a support group allows individuals to connect with others who are facing similar challenges and share coping strategies in a supportive environment.

Options for Professional Support (continued):

1. Crisis Helplines and Hotlines: Numerous phone, text, and online chat services are available to provide immediate support and connect individuals with resources during times of crisis.

2. Integrated Care: Some healthcare settings offer integrated care, which combines primary healthcare services with mental health services to address multiple needs simultaneously.

3. Employee Assistance Programs (EAPs): Many employers provide EAPs, which offer confidential counselling and referral services for employees facing personal or work-related challenges.

4. Educational Institutions: Schools, colleges, and universities often have counselling centres or mental health services available for students, faculty, and staff.

Benefits of Seeking Professional Help:

1. Personalised Treatment Plan: Mental health professionals can assess an individual's unique needs and create a personalised treatment plan to address specific challenges.

2. Improved Coping Skills: Therapy can help individuals learn and practise healthy coping skills to manage stress and other life challenges effectively.

3. Enhanced Self-Awareness: Professional support can increase self-awareness, helping individuals better understand their thoughts, emotions, and behaviours.

4. Stigma Reduction: Seeking professional help contributes to reducing the stigma associated with mental health issues, promoting a more open and accepting environment.

How to Find Professional Help:

1. Referrals: Consult with a primary care provider, trusted friends, or family members for recommendations.

2. Online Resources: Use online databases, directories, or mental health organisations' websites to locate professionals in your area.

3. Insurance Coverage: Contact your health insurance provider to learn about mental health coverage and in-network providers.

Chapter 6

6.0 Physical Well-Being

Physical well-being is an important aspect of overall health and is closely interconnected with mental and emotional well-being. Prioritising and maintaining physical health can have a positive impact on various aspects of life, including mood, energy levels, and resilience.

Key Components of Physical Well-Being:

1. Regular Exercise: Engaging in physical activity, such as aerobic exercise, strength training, or flexibility exercises, can improve cardiovascular health, muscle strength, and endurance.

2. Balanced Nutrition: Consuming a balanced diet rich in fruits, vegetables, lean proteins, whole grains, and healthy fats provides essential nutrients for optimal health.

3. Adequate Sleep: Achieving 7-9 hours of quality sleep each night supports physical health, mental alertness, and emotional well-being.

4. Regular Health Check-Ups: Scheduling routine medical appointments for preventive care, screenings, and vaccinations helps monitor and maintain overall health.

2. Stress Management: Implementing stress management techniques, such as mindfulness and relaxation exercises, can reduce the physical toll of stress on the body.

Benefits of Physical Well-Being:

1. Improved Mood: Regular exercise and proper nutrition can positively influence mood by releasing endorphins and supporting neurotransmitter balance.

2. Enhanced Energy Levels: Prioritising physical well-being can increase energy levels, allowing individuals to engage more fully in daily activities and pursuits.

3. Reduced Risk of Chronic Health Conditions: Maintaining a healthy lifestyle can help prevent or manage chronic health conditions, such as obesity, type 2 diabetes, and cardiovascular disease.

4. Improved Cognitive Function: Regular physical activity and proper nutrition can enhance cognitive function, memory, and focus, benefiting academic or professional performance.

Strategies for Improving Physical Well-Being:

1. Establish a Routine: Develop a consistent exercise schedule and meal plan to maintain healthy habits and ensure adequate physical activity and nutrition.

2. Set Realistic Goals: Create specific, achievable short-term and long-term goals for physical well-being, such as increasing daily step count or incorporating more fruits and vegetables into meals.

3.Monitor Progress: Track progress using tools like fitness trackers or food diaries to stay motivated and identify areas for improvement.

4. Prioritise Self-Care: Engage in activities that promote physical well-being, such as hiking, biking, or practising yoga, and schedule time for relaxation and stress management.

Promoting physical well-being through regular exercise, balanced nutrition, adequate sleep, and stress management is essential for maintaining overall health and enhancing quality of life.

6.1. The Connection Between Body and Mind

The connection between the body and mind is a profound and intricate relationship that significantly influences our overall health and well-being. These two aspects of our being are deeply intertwined, with each impacting and being impacted by the other in various ways.

The Mind-Body Connection

1. Psychological Impact on Physical Health: Our mental and emotional states can significantly affect our physical health. For instance, prolonged stress can weaken the immune system, increase inflammation, and contribute to the development of chronic health conditions.

2. Physical Impact on Mental Health: Physical health and lifestyle factors can influence mental well-being. Regular exercise, balanced nutrition, and adequate sleep can help reduce anxiety, depression, and other mental health issues.

3. Stress Response: The body's response to stress involves the release of hormones, such as cortisol and adrenaline, which prepare us to handle perceived threats. However, chronic activation of this response can negatively impact both physical and mental health.

4. Neuroplasticity: The brain's ability to adapt and change in response to experiences and environmental stimuli highlights the interconnectedness of the mind and body. Mental activities, such as mindfulness and cognitive-behavioural techniques, can reshape brain structure and function.

Cultivating a Healthy Mind-Body Balance

1. Mind-Body Therapies: Engaging in therapies that combine mental and physical health practices, such as yoga, tai chi, or mindfulness-based stress reduction, can help foster a harmonious connection between body and mind.

2. Regular Exercise: Physical activity has been shown to improve mood, reduce stress, and enhance cognitive function, emphasising the link between body and mind.

3. Balanced Nutrition: Proper nutrition provides the essential nutrients needed for optimal brain function and overall physical health, supporting a healthy mind-body connection.

4. Stress Management: Managing stress through relaxation techniques, such as deep breathing or progressive muscle relaxation, can promote a healthy balance between body and mind.

5. Mindful Awareness: Practising mindfulness can help increase self-awareness, enabling individuals to recognize the interconnectedness of their physical, mental, and emotional experiences.

Recognizing and nurturing the connection between body and mind is crucial for achieving optimal health and well-being. By prioritising practices that support both physical and mental health, individuals can foster a strong mind-body connection and experience the benefits of overall wellness.

6.2. Importance of Exercise and Nutrition

Maximising the benefits of exercise and nutrition can not only improve overall health but also contribute to increased productivity, leading to greater profitability in various aspects of life. Here's a detailed explanation of how focusing on exercise and nutrition can boost productivity .

1. Improved Physical Health: Engaging in regular exercise and consuming a balanced diet can significantly enhance physical health by improving cardiovascular fitness, building muscle strength, and supporting immune function. A healthier workforce, for instance, translates to fewer sick days, lower healthcare costs, and higher productivity.

2. Enhanced Cognitive Function: Exercise and proper nutrition have been shown to boost cognitive function, memory, and focus. This mental sharpness can contribute to improved problem-solving, creativity, and decision-making abilities, ultimately leading to greater success in the workplace or academic settings.

3. Elevated Mood and Emotional Well-being: Physical activity releases endorphins, which can help alleviate stress, anxiety, and depression, promoting a more positive outlook and increased resilience. A happier, more optimistic mindset can improve interpersonal relationships, teamwork, and overall job satisfaction, fostering a more productive work environment.

4. Increased Energy and Stamina: Regular exercise and a balanced diet rich in essential nutrients provide the body with the fuel needed to maintain optimal energy levels throughout the day. Increased energy and stamina can help individuals work more efficiently and accomplish more tasks in a given time frame.

5. Improved Time Management: Prioritising exercise and healthy eating habits often necessitates better time management skills. Incorporating these practices into daily routines encourages individuals to become more organised and efficient, which can translate to improved productivity in other areas of life.

6. Long-Term Health and Longevity: Investing in exercise and proper nutrition can contribute to long-term health and well-being, reducing the risk of chronic diseases and promoting longevity. In the long run, this can result in cost savings on medical expenses and a higher quality of life.

Incorporating regular exercise and a balanced diet into daily life can lead to a multitude of benefits, including increased productivity and profitability. By prioritizing physical and mental well-being, individuals can experience greater success in various aspects of life, fostering a healthier and more prosperous future.

Nutrition's Role in Physical Fitness:

1. Proper nutrition is important to maximise athletic performance. Without enough carbohydrates, proteins, and fats, athletes may feel sluggish during workouts or ravenously hungry.

2. Athletes should focus on specific vitamins and minerals for fitness performance, such as iron, vitamin D, and zinc.

3. Consulting with a sports dietitian can help tailor nutrition recommendations to your individual needs and activity level. Evidence Shows Proper Nutrition Supports Activity.

4. Integrating both nutrition and physical activity produces greater benefits than focusing on one alone. Exercise informs food choices, and active individuals tend to make more nutritious decisions. Nutrition may also support muscle recovery by reducing inflammation.

Macronutrients for Optimal Exercise Performance:
1. **Carbohydrates:** Our bodies' preferred source of fuel. They provide energy for daily activities and enhance workouts.
2. **Protein:** Crucial for muscle building, repair, and recovery after exercise.

3. Fat: Keeps us satisfied, cushions bones and joints, and aids in absorbing fat-soluble vitamins (A, E, D, K).

Balanced diet accompanied by regular exercise contributes not only to physical health but also mental well-being. It's a powerful combination.

6.3. Sleep and Its Role in Mental Health

Sleep plays a crucial role in maintaining mental health, contributing to emotional well-being, cognitive function, and overall quality of life. Understanding the importance of sleep and its connection to mental health can help individuals prioritise healthy sleep habits and improve their well-being.

The Sleep-Mental Health Connection

1. Emotional Regulation: Sleep helps regulate emotions by allowing the brain to process daily experiences and consolidate memories. During sleep, the brain evaluates emotional information, helping individuals respond more appropriately to emotional stimuli when awake. Insufficient sleep can lead to increased emotional reactivity, irritability, and mood swings.

2. Cognitive Function: Quality sleep supports various cognitive functions, including memory consolidation, decision-making, and problem-solving. Sleep deprivation can impair cognitive performance, leading to difficulties with attention, learning, and creativity.

3. Mental Health Disorders: Sleep disturbances, such as insomnia or sleep apnea, are often associated with mental health conditions like depression, anxiety, and bipolar disorder. Treating sleep issues may help alleviate symptoms and improve overall mental health.

4. Stress Response: Sleep plays a vital role in regulating the body's stress response system. Lack of sleep can lead to increased cortisol levels, a stress hormone that negatively impacts mood, immune function, and overall health.

5. Suicide Prevention: Research suggests that sleep problems may increase the risk of suicidal thoughts and behaviors. By addressing sleep issues, mental health professionals can potentially contribute to suicide prevention efforts.

Promoting Healthy Sleep Habits

1. Sleep Hygiene: Practise good sleep hygiene by establishing a consistent sleep schedule, creating a relaxing sleep environment, and avoiding stimulating activities before bedtime.

2. Exercise: Regular physical activity can promote better sleep quality, although it's best to avoid vigorous exercise close to bedtime, as it may interfere with sleep onset.

3. Diet: Consuming a balanced diet and limiting caffeine, alcohol, and large meals before bedtime can help support healthy sleep patterns.

4. Stress Management: Engaging in stress management techniques, such as meditation, deep breathing exercises, or yoga, can help create a more relaxed mindset conducive to quality sleep.

5. Professional Help: If sleep issues persist despite making lifestyle changes, seeking professional help from a healthcare provider or a sleep specialist may be necessary to address potential underlying issues and develop a targeted treatment plan.

Bidirectional Connection:

Mental health influences our thoughts, feelings, and actions. It impacts our ability to handle stress, relate to others, and make choices. sleep quality significantly affects mental well-being. Poor sleep can worsen mental health conditions, while mental health problems may lead to sleep disturbances.

1. Brain Activity During Sleep:

Brain activity fluctuates during different sleep stages. Each stage plays a role in brain health, affecting thinking, learning, and memory.

REM (rapid eye movement) sleep is crucial for processing emotional information. Lack of sleep harms positive emotional consolidation, influencing mood and emotional reactivity.

Research suggests that sleep problems can be both a cause and consequence of mental health issues1.

2. Obstructive Sleep Apnea (OSA):

OSA, characterised by breathing pauses during sleep, impacts mental health. Reduced oxygen levels disrupt sleep, affecting overall well-being1.

prioritising good sleep habits contributes to better mental health. Sleep is important component of mental health, influencing emotional regulation, cognitive function, and overall well-being. By prioritising healthy sleep habits and seeking professional help when necessary, individuals can enhance their mental health and enjoy a higher quality of life.

6.4. Building Healthy Habits

Building healthy habits is an essential aspect of personal growth and overall well-being. By developing and maintaining positive habits, individuals can improve their physical health, emotional resilience, and mental well-being. Here are some key strategies for building healthy habits that last.

1. Set Realistic Goals: Begin by establishing clear, achievable goals that align with your priorities and values. Break larger goals into smaller, manageable steps to avoid feeling overwhelmed or discouraged.

2. Create a Routine: Develop a consistent daily or weekly routine that incorporates your desired healthy habits. Establishing a structured schedule can help solidify new habits and make them a natural part of your day-to-day life.

3. Start Small: Focus on making small, incremental changes rather than drastic transformations. Gradual progress is more sustainable and can help build momentum as you work toward your goals.

4. Find Accountability: Enlist the support of a friend, family member, or coach to hold you accountable and provide encouragement as you work on building new habits. Alternatively, consider joining a support group or online community for additional motivation and guidance.

5. Monitor Progress: Track your progress using a journal, app, or planner to stay motivated and identify areas for improvement. Celebrating small wins along the way can help sustain motivation and reinforce positive habits.

6. Make It Enjoyable: Find ways to make your new habits enjoyable and rewarding. For example, listen to music or a podcast while exercising or try new, healthy recipes to keep mealtime interesting.

7. Practice Self-Compassion: Be kind to yourself and practice self-compassion when setbacks occur. Acknowledge that setbacks are a natural part of the process and focus on getting back on track rather than dwelling on mistakes.

8. Stay Flexible: Be open to adapting your habits as your needs and circumstances change. Building healthy habits is an ongoing process that requires flexibility and persistence.

Examples of healthy habits to consider include:

1. Regular physical activity

2. Balanced nutrition
3. Adequate sleep
4. Stress management techniques
5. Positive thinking and self-talk
6. Hydration - Self-care practices
6. Practising gratitude

Implementing these strategies and focusing on building healthy habits, individuals can positively impact their overall well-being, increasing their resilience, and improving their quality of life.

Chapter 7

7.0 Education and Career

Education and career are interconnected aspects of personal and professional growth, influencing an individual's overall well-being, financial stability, and opportunities for advancement. Exploring the relationship between education and career can help individuals make informed decisions about their educational pursuits and professional goals.

Education and Career Development

1. Foundational Skills: Education provides individuals with fundamental skills, such as critical thinking, problem-solving, communication, and teamwork, which are essential for success in various careers.

2. Specialised Knowledge: Pursuing a specific field of study allows individuals to acquire in-depth knowledge and expertise in their chosen area, making them more competitive candidates for relevant job opportunities.

3. Networking Opportunities: Participating in educational programs, internships, or extracurricular activities can help individuals establish connections with peers and professionals, expanding their network and opening doors to potential career opportunities.

4. Career Advancement: Continuing education, professional certifications, or advanced degrees can equip individuals with new skills and knowledge, enabling career growth and higher earning potential.

Education and Career Choices

1. Aligning Interests and Strengths: Selecting an educational path that aligns with one's interests, strengths, and values can lead to a more fulfilling and successful career.

2. Exploring Career Options: Researching various careers and their respective educational requirements can help individuals make informed decisions about their course of study and professional goals.

3. Lifelong Learning: Embracing lifelong learning and staying current with industry trends and developments can support career adaptability and resilience, particularly in rapidly evolving industries.

Balancing Education and Career

1. **Work-Life Balance:** Balancing educational pursuits, career development, and personal life can be challenging but is essential for maintaining overall well-being. Prioritising time for self-care, hobbies, and social connections can help prevent burnout and foster a sense of balance.

2. **Financial Considerations:** Evaluating the cost of education, potential return on investment, and financial aid or scholarship opportunities can help individuals make informed decisions about their educational pursuits and career choices.

3. **Career and Education Resources:** Utilising career counselling, mentorship, or job placement services can provide valuable guidance and support in navigating the relationship between education and career.

7.1. Navigating Academic Pressures

Navigating academic pressures is important for students' well-being and success, as it enables them to cope effectively with various challenges they face during their educational journey.

Understanding Academic Pressures

Academic pressures can manifest in various ways, including:

1.High Expectations: Students often face pressure to meet high academic standards set by parents, teachers, or themselves.

2. Time Management: Juggling coursework, extracurricular activities, and personal life can lead to feelings of overwhelm and stress.

3. Competition: In competitive environments, students may struggle with the pressure to excel and fear of failure.

4. Financial Pressures: The cost of education and the burden of student loans can create additional stress.

5. Social Pressures: Students must also navigate social dynamics and relationships with peers, which can be challenging and distracting.

Strategies for Navigating Academic Pressures

2.Time Management: Prioritising tasks, creating a balanced schedule, and using organisational tools can help students manage their time effectively.

3.Self-Care: Practising healthy habits, such as regular exercise, proper nutrition, and sufficient sleep, can improve physical and mental well-being.

4. Seeking Support: Students can benefit from seeking guidance from academic advisors, counsellors, or mentors for academic and personal challenges.

5. Effective Study Techniques: Implementing efficient study strategies, such as spaced repetition, active recall, and interleaving, can enhance learning and reduce study-related stress.

6. Balanced Extracurricular Involvement: Participating in a manageable number of extracurricular activities can help students maintain a balanced lifestyle while exploring interests outside the classroom.

7. Building a Supportive Peer Network: Connecting with like-minded peers who share similar goals and values can create a sense of belonging and reduce social pressures.

8. Maintaining Perspective: Recognizing that academic performance does not define self-worth can help students approach challenges with resilience and maintain a healthy perspective.

By implementing these strategies, students can navigate academic pressures more effectively, ensuring their well-being, and success both inside and outside the classroom.

Here are some expert tips to help you on your academic journey:

1. Mindful Meditation for Focus:

Mindful meditation is an effective practice that can help improve focus and concentration, reduce stress, and enhance overall well-being. By intentionally bringing awareness to the present moment and observing thoughts, emotions, and sensations without judgement, individuals can cultivate a more focused and balanced state of mind.

Key Principles of Mindful Meditation:

i. Non-judgmental Observation: Observe thoughts, feelings, and sensations as they arise without labelling them as good or bad.

ii. Present Moment Awareness: Focus on the present moment, rather than dwelling on the past or worrying about the future.

iii. Acceptance: Accept thoughts and emotions as they come and go without attempting to suppress or change them.

Steps for Practising Mindful Meditation for Focus

i. Find a Quiet Space: Choose a quiet, comfortable space free from distractions where you can sit or lie down without being disturbed.

ii. Get Comfortable: Assume a relaxed posture, either sitting or lying down, and close your eyes or soften your gaze.

iii. Breath Awareness: Focus your attention on your breath, noticing the sensations of air flowing in and out of your nostrils or the rise and fall of your chest or abdomen.

iv. Non-judgmental Observation: Observe your thoughts and emotions as they arise without engaging or judging them. Gently redirect your focus back to your breath when you notice your mind wandering.

2. Gamify Your Learning: Gamification is a powerful technique that can make learning more engaging, enjoyable, and effective. By incorporating game-like elements into the learning process, individuals can increase motivation, improve retention, and enhance overall learning outcomes.

Sme strategies for gamifying your learning:

i. Set Clear Goals and Objective: Establish specific learning goals or milestones and track your progress as you work toward achieving them. This can provide a sense of purpose and accomplishment, much like completing levels in a game.

ii. Friendly Competition: Engage in friendly competition with peers or classmates to encourage motivation and push yourself to learn more effectively. This can be done through group study sessions, quizzes, or other learning challenges.

iii. Interactive Learning Tools: Utilise interactive learning tools, such as educational apps, online quizzes, or game-based learning platforms, to make the learning process more dynamic and enjoyable.

iv. Point Systems: Assign points for completing tasks, achieving milestones, or demonstrating mastery of new concepts. Keep track of your points and try to beat your previous scores or compete with friends.

3. Diversify Learning Environments:

Don't just stick to traditional study spaces.
Explore different locations on and off campus—Purdue and Chauncey Hill are filled with parks, coffee shops, and co-working spaces.
A change in scenery can stimulate your focus and avoid burnout from working in one place.

4. Utilise Learning Technologies:

Virtual reality (VR) and augmented reality (AR) applications aren't just limited to headsets anymore. Platforms like Studyverse or VRChat offer virtual study rooms, providing connection with other students, with or without the headgear.

5. Artistic Expression for Concept Mastery:
Creative outlets can solidify your understanding of complex concepts.

Try sketchnotes, visual diagrams, or even mnemonics and songs related to course material. These alternative pathways enhance memory retention and conceptual understanding.

7.2. Career Planning in a Changing World

Career planning in today's rapidly evolving world requires adaptability, foresight, and a commitment to lifelong learning. As technological advancements, globalisation, and economic shifts continue to reshape the job market, individuals must be prepared to navigate these changes effectively to achieve career success.

Key Considerations for Career Planning

1. Emerging Industries and Job Roles: Staying informed about emerging industries, such as renewable energy, artificial intelligence, and biotechnology, can help individuals identify potential career paths and skill requirements.

2. Lifelong Learning: Embracing a growth mindset and engaging in continuous learning is essential for adapting to changes in the job market and maintaining employability.

3. Transferable Skills: Developing skills that can be applied across various roles and industries, such as communication, problem-solving, and leadership, is crucial for long-term career success.

4. Networking: Building and maintaining a strong professional network can provide valuable connections, insights, and opportunities for career advancement.

5. Work-Life Balance: Prioritising work-life balance and personal well-being can help individuals sustain long-term career success and satisfaction.

Strategies for Career Planning in a Changing World

1. Conducting Research: Stay informed about industry trends, job market forecasts, and in-demand skills to guide career decision-making and professional development efforts.

2. Setting SMART Goals: Establish Specific, Measurable, Achievable, Relevant, and Time-bound career goals to provide direction and focus.

3. Building a Diverse Skill Set: Develop a wide range of technical and soft skills that can be applied across various roles and industries.

4. Seeking Mentorship: Seek guidance from experienced professionals to gain valuable insights, feedback, and advice for navigating career challenges and opportunities.

5. Developing a Personal Brand: Cultivate a unique personal brand that highlights your skills, achievements, and professional values to stand out in the job market.

7.3. Balancing Ambition with Well-Being

Striking a balance between ambition and well-being is essential for leading a fulfilling and successful life. While ambition drives individuals to set and achieve goals, it is equally important to prioritise mental and physical health to maintain long-term well-being.

Potential Challenges

1. Burnout: Over-emphasizing ambition can lead to burnout, characterised by exhaustion, cynicism, and reduced productivity.

2. Neglecting Personal Life: Excessive focus on career goals may result in neglecting relationships, hobbies, and self-care.

3. Unrealistic Expectations: Setting unattainable goals can lead to frustration, disappointment, and self-doubt.

4. Comparison and Competition: Comparing oneself to others and engaging in unhealthy competition can negatively impact self-esteem and well-being.

Strategies for Balancing Ambition with Well-Being

1. Establish Boundaries: Set clear boundaries between work and personal life to prevent work from encroaching on leisure time and relationships.

2. Prioritise Self-Care: Make time for activities that promote physical and mental well-being, such as exercise, meditation, and engaging in hobbies. -

3. Set Realistic Goals: Ensure that goals are specific, achievable, and aligned with personal values to maintain motivation and prevent burnout.

For more Strategies for Balancing Ambition with Well-Being consider this

1. Practice Mindfulness: Cultivate mindfulness to stay present and aware of thoughts, emotions, and physical sensations. This can help individuals recognize when their ambition may be negatively impacting their well-being.

2. Foster Supportive Relationships: Surround oneself with supportive friends, family, or mentors who encourage a healthy balance between ambition and well-being.

3. Focus on Personal Growth: Emphasise learning, growth, and self-improvement, rather than solely on external achievements and recognition.

Balancing ambition with well-being is key to achieving lasting success and happiness. By setting realistic goals, prioritising self-care, and maintaining healthy relationships, individuals can pursue their ambitions while also nurturing their mental and physical health.

7.4. Lifelong Learning and Growth

Lifelong learning and growth are important components of personal development and career success. In a world characterised by constant change, individuals must continuously adapt, acquire new skills, and broaden their knowledge to remain competitive and find fulfilment.

Benefits of Lifelong Learning and Growth

1. Enhanced Employability: Acquiring new skills and knowledge can increase job opportunities and ensure individuals remain relevant in the changing job market.

2. Improved Mental Health: Learning stimulates the brain, promotes cognitive function, and can contribute to overall mental well-being.

3. Personal Fulfilment: Pursuing personal interests and passions through learning can lead to a greater sense of fulfilment and purpose

Consider this for more Benefits of Lifelong Learning and Growth

1. Expanded Perspective: Exposure to diverse ideas, experiences, and cultures through learning promotes empathy, understanding, and a broader worldview.

2. Increased Adaptability: Embracing a growth mindset and a commitment to lifelong learning fosters adaptability and resilience in the face of change.

Strategies for Lifelong Learning and Growth

1. Setting Learning Goals: Identify specific skills or areas of knowledge to pursue and develop a plan to achieve these goals.

2. Embracing Diverse Learning Opportunities: Take advantage of various learning formats, such as online courses, workshops, seminars, and self-directed learning.

3. Engaging in Professional Development: Pursue professional development opportunities, such as industry conferences, certifications, or mentorship programs, to enhance career growth.

4. Fostering Curiosity: Cultivate a sense of curiosity and actively seek new knowledge, ideas, and experiences.

Follow this for more Strategies for Lifelong Learning and Growth

1. Building a Learning Community: Connect with like-minded individuals who share a passion for learning and growth.

2. Reflection and Self-Awareness: Regularly reflect on personal strengths, weaknesses, and areas for improvement to guide ongoing learning and development.

3. Embracing a Growth Mindset: View challenges and failures as opportunities for growth and development, rather than as setbacks.

lifelong learning and growth are important for personal and professional fulfilment. embracing diverse learning opportunities, fostering curiosity, and cultivating a growth mindset, individuals can continuously adapt, evolve, and thrive in a rapidly changing world.

Chapter 8

8.0 Digital Detox

A digital detox can be incredibly beneficial, especially in today's hyper-connected world. The goal is to reduce stress, improve mental health, and reconnect with the physical world. In the context of Generation Z, who are often highly connected to digital devices, a digital detox can be particularly beneficial.

Benefits of a Digital Detox

Here are some detailed strategies to help you incorporate a digital detox into your routine:

1. Understanding Digital Detox
A digital detox involves taking a break from digital devices like smartphones, computers, and tablets to reduce stress and improve mental well-being. It's about finding a balance between online and offline activities.

2. Reduced Anxiety: Constant notifications and the pressure to stay connected can lead to heightened anxiety levels. By taking a break from digital devices, individuals can experience a significant reduction in stress and anxiety. This break allows the mind to rest and recover from the constant influx of information. A digital detox helps reduce this stress.

3. Improved Sleep: Exposure to blue light from screens can interfere with the production of melatonin, the hormone responsible for regulating sleep. Reducing screen time, especially before bedtime, can lead to better sleep quality and overall health.

4. Enhanced Focus and Productivity: Digital devices can be a major source of distraction. limiting their use, individuals can improve their concentration and productivity. This is particularly important for students and professionals who need to focus on their tasks without constant interruptions. Taking breaks from digital devices can improve concentration and productivity.

4. Better Relationships: Spending less time on digital devices allows for more meaningful interactions with family and friends. Face-to-face communication can strengthen relationships and improve social skills, which are essential for emotional well-being.

Strategies for a Successful Digital Detox

1. Create a Schedule: Plan specific times when you will be offline. Start with small intervals, such as an hour a day, and gradually increase the duration. Consistency is key to making a digital detox a regular part of your routine.

2. Designate Device-Free Zones: Establish areas in your home where digital devices are not allowed, such as the dining room or bedroom. This helps create a physical separation between you and your devices, making it easier to disconnect.

3. Engage in Offline Activities: Find hobbies and activities that don't involve screens, such as Reading, exercising, cooking, and spending time outdoors are great ways to enjoy your time without relying on digital devices.

For More Strategies for a Successful Digital Detox consider this

1. Use Technology to Your Advantage: There are apps designed to help you monitor and limit your screen time. Use these tools to stay on track and make your digital detox more manageable.

2. Inform Others: Let friends and family know about your digital detox so they can support you and understand your reduced online presence. This can also encourage them to join you in taking a break from digital devices.

3. Reflect and Adjust: Regularly assess how the detox is impacting your well-being and make adjustments as needed. If you find certain strategies aren't working, try new ones until you find what works best for you.

Practical Tips for Daily Life

1. Start Small: Begin with short digital detox periods, like an hour a day, and gradually increase the time. This makes the process less overwhelming and more sustainable.

2. Mindful Usage: Be conscious of your digital habits. Use devices intentionally rather than mindlessly scrolling through social media or other apps.

3. Unplug Before Bed: Establish a routine to disconnect from screens at least an hour before bedtime. This can improve sleep quality and help you wind down more effectively.

4. Digital Sabbaticals: Consider taking longer breaks, such as a weekend or a week, to fully recharge. Use this time to engage in activities that you enjoy and that help you relax.

Incorporating Digital Detox into Daily Life

1. Morning Routine: Start your day without checking your phone. Use this time for meditation, exercise, or a healthy breakfast.

2. Work Breaks: Take regular breaks from screens during work hours. Step outside, stretch, or have a face-to-face conversation with a colleague. These breaks can help reduce eye strain and improve focus.

3. Evening Wind-Down: Spend your evenings engaging in relaxing activities that don't involve screens, such as reading a book, taking a walk, or practising a hobby. This can help you unwind and prepare for a restful night's sleep.

Incorporating these strategies, you can effectively manage your digital consumption and enhance your overall well-being. A digital detox can be a powerful tool in building resilience and reducing anxiety, especially for Generation Z.

8.1. Managing Screen Time

Managing screen time is important in today's digital age, especially for Generation Z, who are constantly surrounded by technology. Here are some detailed strategies to help manage screen time effectively.

Set Clear Boundaries and Rules: Establishing clear rules about when and where screens can be used is essential. For example, no screens during meals or an hour before bedtime.

2. Encourage Alternative Activities: Promote activities that don't involve screens, such as reading, outdoor sports, or hobbies like painting and playing musical instruments. This helps in reducing dependency on digital devices and encourages a balanced lifestyle.

3. Use Technology Wisely: Leverage parental controls and apps that monitor and limit screen time. These tools can help manage the content and duration of screen usage, ensuring it remains within healthy limits.

4. Model Good Behaviour: Children and teens often mimic the behaviour of adults. By setting a good example and limiting your own screen time, you can encourage them to do the same.

5. Create Tech-Free Zones: Designate certain areas of the home as tech-free zones, such as bedrooms and dining areas. This helps in creating a physical separation from screens and promotes more face-to-face interactions.

6. Schedule Screen Time: Instead of allowing unrestricted access, schedule specific times for screen use. This can help in managing expectations and reducing the impulse to use screens constantly.

7. Educate About the Impact: Teach children and teens about the potential negative effects of excessive screen time, such as eye strain, sleep disturbances, and reduced physical activity. Awareness can motivate them to self-regulate their screen usage.

8. Encourage Social Interaction: Promote real-life social interactions over virtual ones. Encourage participation in group activities, clubs, or sports that require face-to-face communication.

9. Monitor Content: Be aware of what content is being consumed. Ensure that it is age-appropriate and educational. Discuss the content with them to understand their interests and guide them towards healthier choices.

10. Balance Screen Time with Physical Activity: Ensure that screen time is balanced with adequate physical activity. Encourage regular breaks and physical exercises to counteract the sedentary nature of screen use4.

8.2. Social Media, whatFriend or Foe

Social Media as a Friend

1. Enhanced Communication and Connectivity

i. Global Reach: Social media platforms like Facebook, Instagram, and Twitter allow people to stay connected with friends and family, regardless of geographical distances. This can be particularly valuable for maintaining relationships and fostering a sense of community.

ii. Instant Communication: Features like instant messaging, video calls, and group chats make it easier to stay in touch and share experiences in real-time.

2. Access to Information and Resources

i. Educational Content: Social media provides a wealth of information at our fingertips. Users can follow news outlets, industry experts, and educational pages to stay informed about current events and trends. Platforms like YouTube and LinkedIn offer a plethora of educational videos, webinars, and courses on various topics, from academic subjects to professional skills. This can be especially beneficial for professional development and learning.

ii. News and Updates: Social media is a quick way to stay updated with the latest news, trends, and developments in various fields. Following reputable news sources and experts can provide valuable insights.

3. Support Networks

i. Online communities and support groups: Online communities and support groups can offer emotional support and practical advice. For individuals dealing with mental health issues, chronic illnesses, or other challenges, these groups can provide a sense of belonging and understanding.

ii. Peer Support: For individuals facing challenges, peer support groups on social media can offer emotional support and practical advice, helping them feel less isolated.

4. Platform for Expression and Activism

i. Creative Expression: Social media allows users to share their creativity through photos, videos, writing, and other forms of content. Platforms like Instagram and TikTok are popular for showcasing artistic talents.

ii. Social Activism: Social media has become a powerful tool for raising awareness about social issues, organising events, and mobilising support for causes.

Platform for Expression and Activism Social media gives a voice to individuals and groups who might otherwise be unheard. It can be a powerful tool for raising awareness about social issues, organising events, and mobilising support for causes.

Social Media as a Foe

1. Mental Health Concerns

i. Anxiety and Depression: Studies have shown that excessive use of social media can lead to increased feelings of anxiety and depression. The constant comparison to others' seemingly perfect lives can result in feelings of inadequacy and low self-esteem.

ii. Sleep Disturbances: The blue light emitted by screens can interfere with sleep patterns, leading to poor sleep quality and increased stress.

2. Privacy Issues

i. Data Collection: Social media platforms often collect and share user data for advertising purposes. This can lead to concerns about privacy and the potential misuse of personal information.
ii. Cybersecurity Risks: Users may unknowingly expose personal information that can be exploited by cybercriminals, leading to identity theft and other security issues.

3. Cyberbullying and Harassment

i. Anonymity and Harassment: The anonymity provided by social media can sometimes lead to negative behaviors such as cyberbullying and harassment. Victims of cyberbullying can experience severe emotional and psychological impacts.
ii. Trolling: Negative and inflammatory comments, often referred to as trolling, can create a hostile online environment and affect users' mental well-being.

4. Addictive Nature

i. Engagement Design: Social media platforms are designed to be engaging, which can lead to addictive behaviours. Features like endless scrolling, notifications, and likes are intended to keep users hooked.

ii. Impact on Productivity: Spending excessive time on social media can interfere with daily activities, work, and real-life interactions, leading to decreased productivity and social isolation.

Balancing the Two

To harness the benefits of social media while mitigating its drawbacks, consider the following strategies:

1. Set Time Limits: Use apps or built-in features to monitor and limit your screen time. Setting specific times for social media use can help manage its impact on your daily life.

2. Engage Mindfully: Be conscious of how you feel when using social media and take breaks if you start to feel overwhelmed. Mindful engagement can help you use social media in a healthier way.

3. Protect Your Privacy: Regularly review privacy settings and be cautious about the information you share online. Ensuring your personal information is secure can reduce the risk of privacy issues.

4. Promote Real-Life Interactions: Encourage face-to-face interactions and activities that don't involve screens. Balancing online and offline interactions can help maintain healthy relationships and well-being.

Being mindful of how we use social media, we can maximise its benefits and minimise its potential harms. This balanced approach can help Generation Z navigate the digital landscape more effectively, reducing anxiety and promoting resilience.

Effects of Social Media

1. Positive Effects

i. Enhanced Learning Opportunities: Social media platforms like LinkedIn Learning, Coursera, and even YouTube offer a wide range of educational content. This makes learning more accessible and flexible, allowing users to acquire new skills and knowledge at their own pace.

ii. Increased Awareness and Advocacy: Social media has been instrumental in raising awareness about important social issues. Campaigns like BlackLivesMatter and ClimateStrike has gained global attention and mobilised millions of people to take action.

iii. Networking and Career Opportunities: Platforms like LinkedIn provide valuable networking opportunities, helping users connect with industry professionals, find job opportunities, and advance their careers.

2. Negative Effects

I. Distraction and Reduced Productivity: Social media can be highly distracting, leading to procrastination and reduced productivity. The constant notifications and the urge to check updates can interfere with work and study.

ii. Sleep Disruption: The blue light emitted by screens can disrupt sleep patterns, leading to poor sleep quality and increased stress. Late-night scrolling can also delay bedtime and reduce overall sleep duration.

Benefits of Social Media

1. Social Connectivity

i. Maintaining Relationships: Social media helps people stay connected with friends and family, regardless of geographical distances. This can strengthen relationships and provide emotional support.

ii. Building Communities: Online communities and groups allow people with similar interests or challenges to connect, share experiences, and support each other. This can create a sense of belonging and reduce feelings of isolation.

2. Access to Information and Resources

i. Educational Content: Social media platforms offer a wealth of educational resources, from tutorials and webinars to articles and e-books. This makes it easier for users to learn new skills and stay informed about various topics.

ii. Health and Wellness: Many social media accounts focus on health and wellness, providing tips on fitness, nutrition, mental health, and more. This can help users adopt healthier lifestyles and improve their well-being.

3. Professional Development

i. Networking Opportunities: Platforms like LinkedIn allow users to connect with industry professionals, join professional groups, and participate in discussions. This can enhance career prospects and provide valuable insights into various fields.

ii. Job Search and Recruitment: Social media has become a powerful tool for job searching and recruitment. Companies often post job openings on their social media pages, and users can showcase their skills and experience to potential employers.

4. Creative Expression and Entertainment

i. Showcasing Talent: Social media provides a platform for users to showcase their talents, whether it's photography, writing, music, or art. This can lead to recognition, opportunities, and even monetization of their skills.

ii. Entertainment: Social media offers a wide range of entertainment options, from funny videos and memes to live streams and virtual events. This can provide a much-needed break and help users relax and unwind.

Balancing the Effects and Benefits

To maximize the benefits of social media while minimizing its negative effects, consider the following strategies.

1. Mindful Usage: Be aware of how much time you spend on social media and how it affects your mood and productivity. Set specific times for social media use and take regular breaks.

2. Positive Engagement: Follow accounts that inspire and uplift you, and engage in positive interactions. Avoid negative or toxic content that can affect your mental well-being.

3. Privacy Protection: Regularly review your privacy settings and be cautious about the information you share online. Protecting your personal information can reduce the risk of privacy issues.

4. Healthy Balance: Balance your online activities with offline ones. Engage in physical activities, hobbies, and face-to-face interactions to maintain a healthy lifestyle.

Adopting these strategies, you can enjoy the benefits of social media while mitigating its potential harms, leading to a more balanced and fulfilling digital experience.

8.3. Building Healthy Digital Habits

Building healthy digital habits is important for maintaining mental well-being and productivity, especially in our increasingly digital world. Here are some detailed strategies to help you cultivate these habits.

1. Set Clear Boundaries

i. Designate Tech-Free Times: Establish specific times of the day when you avoid using digital devices, such as during meals, an hour before bedtime, or during family time.

ii. Create Tech-Free Zones: Designate certain areas of your home, like the bedroom or dining room, as tech-free zones to encourage more face-to-face interactions and better sleep hygiene.

2. Prioritise Quality Over Quantity

i. Curate Your Content: Follow accounts and subscribe to channels that provide positive, educational, and inspiring content.

iii. Limit Multitasking: Focus on one digital task at a time to improve productivity and reduce cognitive overload. For example, avoid checking social media while working or studying.

3. Use Technology Mindfully

i. Set Time Limits: Use apps or built-in features on your devices to monitor and limit your screen time.

Setting daily or weekly limits can help you stay within healthy usage boundaries.

ii. Take Regular Breaks: Follow the 20-20-20 rule: every 20 minutes, take a 20-second break and look at something 20 feet away to reduce eye strain and mental fatigue.

4. Engage in Offline Activities

i. Pursue Hobbies: Engage in activities that don't involve screens, such as reading, gardening, painting, or playing a musical instrument. This helps in reducing dependency on digital devices.

ii. Exercise Regularly: Physical activity is crucial for mental and physical health.

Follow this for more strategies to help you cultivate Building healthy digital habits.

1. Practice Digital Detox

i. Scheduled Detox Periods: Plan regular digital detox periods where you completely disconnect from digital devices. This could be a few hours each day, a full day each week, or a weekend each month.

ii. Mindfulness and Meditation: Use the time during your digital detox to practise mindfulness or meditation.

2. Enhance Digital Literacy

i. Stay Informed: Educate yourself about the potential risks and benefits of digital technology. Understanding how algorithms work and how your data is used can help you make more informed decisions.

ii. Teach Digital Etiquette: Promote respectful and responsible behaviour online. Encourage open discussions about digital etiquette and the impact of online actions on others.

3. Monitor and Reflect

i. Track Your Usage: Regularly review your screen time and digital habits. Use this information to identify patterns and areas where you can improve.

ii. Reflect on Your Digital Experience: Take time to reflect on how your digital habits affect your mood, productivity, and relationships. Adjust your habits as needed to align with your goals and values. Implementing these strategies, you can build healthier digital habits that enhance your well-being and productivity. Remember, the goal is to find a balance that works for you and supports a fulfilling, balanced life.

8.4. Disconnecting to Reconnect

Disconnecting to Reconnect is a powerful concept, especially relevant in today's digital age. It involves intentionally stepping away from technology and digital distractions to foster deeper connections with ourselves, others, and the world around us.

The Concept of Disconnecting to Reconnect

1. Digital Detox
A digital detox involves taking a break from digital devices such as smartphones, computers, and tablets. The primary goal is to reduce the stress and anxiety associated with constant connectivity and information overload.

i. Stress Reduction: Continuous exposure to digital screens can lead to eye strain, headaches, and increased stress levels. A digital detox helps alleviate these symptoms by giving your mind and body a chance to rest.

ii. Improved Focus: Without the constant barrage of notifications and alerts, you can concentrate better on tasks, leading to increased productivity and efficiency.

iii. Enhanced Well-being: Taking time away from screens allows you to engage in activities that promote physical and mental health, such as exercise, reading, or spending time outdoors.

2. Mindfulness and Presence

Disconnecting from technology encourages mindfulness, which is the practice of being fully present in the moment. This can lead to a deeper appreciation of your surroundings and experiences.

i. Mindful Living: focusing on the present moment, you can reduce anxiety about the future and regrets about the past. This practice helps cultivate a sense of peace and contentment.

ii. Enhanced Sensory Experience: Without digital distractions, you can fully engage your senses in activities, whether it's savouring a meal, enjoying a walk in nature, or having a meaningful conversation.

3. Mental Health Benefits

Constant connectivity can lead to information overload, increased stress, and a sense of FOMO (Fear of Missing Out). Disconnecting helps mitigate these effects, leading to better mental health.

i. Reduced Anxiety: Taking breaks from social media and news can reduce anxiety and stress levels. It allows you to focus on your own life rather than comparing yourself to others.

ii. Improved Sleep: Exposure to screens before bedtime can disrupt sleep patterns. Disconnecting from devices in the evening promotes better sleep hygiene and overall health.

Practical Strategies for Disconnecting

1. Set Boundaries

Establishing clear boundaries with technology is crucial for a successful digital detox.

i. Scheduled Breaks: Designate specific times of the day to unplug from all digital devices. This could be during meals, before bed, or during family time.

ii. Notification Management: Turn off non-essential notifications to minimise distractions and interruptions throughout the day.

2. Engage in Offline Activities

Finding enjoyable activities that don't involve screens can make the process of disconnecting more enjoyable.

ii. Outdoor Activities: Spend time in nature, go for a hike, or take a walk in the park. These activities can be refreshing and rejuvenating.

ii. Hobbies and Interests: Engage in hobbies such as reading, painting, cooking, or playing a musical instrument. These activities provide a sense of accomplishment and joy.

3. Mindfulness Practices

Incorporating mindfulness practices into your daily routine can help centre your mind and reduce the urge to check your devices.

i. Meditation: Practice meditation to calm your mind and improve focus.

ii. Yoga and Breathing Exercises: These practices promote relaxation and mental clarity, helping you stay grounded and present.

4. Create Tech-Free Zones

Establishing areas in your home where technology is not allowed encourages more face-to-face interactions and better sleep hygiene.

i. Dining Room: Make mealtimes tech-free to foster meaningful conversations and connections with family members.

ii. Bedroom: Keep electronic devices out of the bedroom to promote better sleep and relaxation.

The Importance of Reconnecting

1. Enhanced Creativity
Without the constant barrage of information, our minds have the space to wander and be creative. This can lead to new ideas and solutions.

i. Creative Pursuits: Engage in creative activities such as writing, drawing, or brainstorming. These activities can stimulate your imagination and lead to innovative ideas.

ii. Problem-Solving: A clear and focused mind is better equipped to solve problems and think critically.

2. Better Productivity
Reducing distractions, you can focus better on tasks at hand, leading to increased productivity and efficiency.

i. Time Management: Use techniques such as the Pomodoro Technique to manage your time effectively and stay focused on tasks.

ii. Task Prioritization: Prioritise tasks based on importance and urgency to ensure that you are working on what truly matters.

Chapter 9

9.0 Building Support Networks

Building a strong support network is important for overall well-being and resilience. Whether you're navigating life's challenges, pursuing career goals, or maintaining good mental health, having a reliable network of people you can trust is important. Here are some expert tips on how to build and nurture your support system.

Identify Your Support Needs:
Reflect on your specific needs. Are you seeking emotional support from close family and friends? Or perhaps you're interested in professional advice or expanding your social circle?
Understanding what you require helps you target the right connections.

Family and Friends:

Family: Your family can be an important source of support. Assess the quality of your relationships and lean on those who genuinely care for you.

Friends: Friends offer unique perspectives and can provide support from an outside viewpoint.

Cultivate meaningful friendships.

1. Colleagues and Professional Networks: Colleagues at work can be part of your support system. Share experiences, seek advice, and collaborate. Join professional associations, attend networking events, and connect with like-minded individuals.

2. Community-Based Groups: Explore community organisations, nonprofits, and local centres. These groups often provide emotional and practical support. Attend community events, workshops, and volunteer opportunities.

3. Virtual Communities and Social Media: Engage with online communities related to your interests or challenges.
Platforms like Facebook groups, TikTok, and specialised forums connect people globally.

4. Mutual Support and Reciprocity: Remember that relationships are a two-way street. Offer support to others as well. Be open to giving and receiving assistance—it strengthens connections.

Having access to a strong support network offers numerous benefits:

1. Reduced stress and anxiety.
2. Better sleep quality.
3. Increased resiliency.
4. Improved overall well-being.

Building a support system involves engaging in communities, seeking positive relationships, and being open to asking for and offering help. While others play an important role, don't forget to support yourself through self-care, coping mechanisms, and setting boundaries.

9.1. The Role of Family and Friends

Family and friends play important roles in our lives, providing emotional support, fostering a sense of belonging, and contributing to our overall well-being. Let's explore these roles.

1. Emotional Support

Family: Families offer a stable source of emotional support throughout life. From childhood, family members provide love, care, and encouragement. This support helps individuals navigate life's challenges, build resilience, and develop a sense of security. For example, parents often provide comfort and guidance during difficult times, while siblings can offer companionship and understanding.

Friends: Friends provide a different kind of emotional support. They offer companionship, share interests, and provide a listening ear. Friendships can be particularly valuable during times of stress or change, offering a sense of belonging and understanding. For instance, friends can help you process emotions, offer advice, and provide a sense of normalcy during turbulent times.

2. Sense of Belonging and Identity

Family: Families shape our identity and sense of belonging from a young age. They instil values, traditions, and cultural norms that influence our self-concept and worldview. For example, family traditions during holidays or cultural practices can create a strong sense of identity and continuity.

Friends: Friendships contribute to our social identity. They help us explore different aspects of our personality and provide a sense of community. Friends often share common interests and experiences, reinforcing our sense of belonging. For instance, being part of a friend group with shared hobbies or interests can enhance your sense of identity and community.

3. Socialization and Development

Family: Families are the primary agents of socialisation. They teach us how to interact with others, manage emotions, and develop social skills.

Positive family interactions contribute to emotional regulation, self-confidence, and social competence. For example, family dinners can teach communication skills and foster a sense of togetherness.

Friends: Friendships play a significant role in social development, especially during adolescence and adulthood. They offer opportunities to practise social skills, navigate conflicts, and build interpersonal relationships. For instance, friendships during school years can help develop teamwork, empathy, and conflict resolution skills.

4. Support During Life Transitions

Family: Families provide stability and support during major life transitions, such as moving to a new city, starting a new job, or experiencing loss. Their consistent presence helps individuals adapt to change and maintain a sense of continuity. For example, parents might offer financial support or advice during a career change.

Friends: Friends offer practical and emotional support during transitions. They can provide advice, share experiences, and help ease the stress of new situations. For instance, friends can help you settle into a new city by introducing you to social circles or offering a place to stay.

5. Health and Well-Being

Family: Strong family bonds are associated with better mental and physical health. Supportive family environments reduce the risk of mental health issues and promote overall well-being. For example, family support can encourage healthy lifestyle choices and provide a buffer against stress.

Friends: Friendships also contribute to health and well-being. Social connections reduce feelings of loneliness, increase happiness, and provide a buffer against stress. For instance, regular social interactions with friends can improve mood and reduce the risk of depression.

9.2. Creating a Community of Support

Creating a community of support is important for fostering resilience and reducing anxiety, especially for Generation Z. Here are some strategies to help you build and maintain a supportive community.

Understanding the Importance of Community: A supportive community provides emotional, social, and sometimes even practical support. It can help individuals feel connected, understood, and less isolated. For Generation Z, who often face unique challenges related to digital life, academic pressures, and social dynamics, a strong community can be a crucial source of strength.

Benefits of a Supportive Community Emotional Support

Having people to talk to about your feelings and experiences can significantly reduce stress and anxiety.

1. Shared Resources: Communities often share valuable resources, such as study materials, job opportunities, and mental health resources.

2, Increased Motivation: Being part of a group with similar goals can boost motivation and accountability.

3. Sense of Belonging: Feeling part of a community can enhance self-esteem and provide a sense of belonging.

Strategies for Building a Supportive Community

1. Existing Groups: Look for existing groups that align with your interests and needs. This could be clubs, online forums, support groups, or community organisations. Platforms like Meetup, Facebook

Groups, and local community centres are great places to start.

2. Create Your Own Group: If you can't find a group that meets your needs, consider starting your own. This could be a study group, a book club, or a support group. Use social media and word of mouth to invite people to join.

3. Be Active and Engaged: Participate actively in your community. Attend meetings, contribute to discussions, and offer support to others.

4. Build Trust and Relationships: Take the time to build trust and form meaningful relationships within your community. Be open, honest, and supportive. Trust is the foundation of any strong community.

Here is More Strategies for Building a Supportive Community

1. Offer Help: Be willing to offer help and support to others. This creates a reciprocal relationship where everyone benefits. Helping others can also boost your own sense of purpose and well-being. Utilise

2. Technology: Use technology to stay connected with your community. Online platforms, social media, and messaging apps can help you maintain relationships and stay engaged, even when you can't meet in person.

3. Diverse Connections: Build a diverse community with people from different backgrounds, experiences, and perspectives. This diversity can enrich your understanding and provide a broader range of support.

Practical Tips for Maintaining a Supportive Community

1. Regular Check-Ins: Schedule regular check-ins with your community members. This could be weekly meetings, monthly gatherings, or casual catch-ups.

2. Celebrate Achievements: Celebrate each other's achievements, no matter how small. This fosters a positive and encouraging environment.

3. Create Safe Spaces: Ensure that your community is a safe space where everyone feels comfortable sharing their thoughts and feelings without judgement.

4. Encourage Open Communication: Promote open and honest communication. Encourage members to express their needs and concerns.

5. Adapt and Grow: Be open to change and growth within your community. As needs and circumstances change, adapt your community to continue providing relevant support.

Incorporating Community Support into Daily Life

1. Daily Interactions: Make an effort to interact with your community daily, even if it's just a quick message or a phone call.

2. Support Networks: Identify key people in your support network and make a conscious effort to stay connected with them.

Building and maintaining a supportive community, you can create a network of resilience that helps you navigate the challenges of life.

9.3. Effective Communication Skills

Effective communication skills are interested for building strong relationships, reducing misunderstandings, and enhancing both personal and professional interactions. Here are some strategies to help you improve your communication skills.

1. Understanding Effective Communication: Effective communication is more than just exchanging information. It involves both the sender and receiver being clear, concise, and empathetic in their interactions.

Key Components of Effective Communication:
Active listening: Active listening helps you understand the speaker's perspective and respond appropriately.

2. Non-Verbal Communication: Body language, facial expressions, gestures, and eye contact play a crucial role in communication. Non-verbal cues can reinforce or contradict what is being said, so it's important to be aware of them.

3. Clarity and Conciseness: Be clear and concise in your communication. Avoid using jargon or complex language that might confuse the listener. The goal is to convey your message in the simplest way possible.

4. Empathy: Understanding and sharing the feelings of others can help build stronger connections. Empathy allows you to respond in a way that acknowledges the other person's emotions and perspectives.

5. Open-Mindedness: Be open to new ideas and perspectives. This helps in creating a more inclusive and respectful communication environment.

Constructive feedback helps improve performance and fosters a culture of continuous improvement.

Strategies to Improve Communication Skills
1. Practise Active Listening: Focus on the speaker, avoid interrupting, and provide feedback by nodding or using verbal affirmations.

2. Be Mindful of Non-Verbal Cues: Pay attention to your body language and that of others. Ensure your non-verbal signals match your words. For example, maintain eye contact and avoid crossing your arms.

3. Use Clear and Concise Language: Avoid unnecessary words and get straight to the point. This helps prevent misunderstandings and keeps the conversation focused.

4. Develop Emotional Intelligence: Work on recognizing and managing your emotions and those of others. This can improve your interactions and help you respond more effectively in various situations.

5. Ask Questions: Asking questions shows that you are engaged and interested in the conversation. It also helps clarify any doubts and ensures a better understanding of the topic.

6. Provide Constructive Feedback: When giving feedback, be specific, focus on the behaviour rather than the person, and offer suggestions for improvement. This makes the feedback more actionable and less personal.

9.4. Leveraging Technology for Positive Connections

Leveraging technology for positive connections can significantly enhance our social interactions, reduce feelings of isolation, and foster a sense of community. Here are some strategies to help you use technology to build and maintain positive connections.

Understanding the Role of Technology: Technology, when used mindfully, can be a powerful tool for creating and sustaining meaningful relationships. It can bridge geographical gaps, provide platforms for shared interests, and offer support networks that might not be available locally.

Benefits of Using Technology for Positive Connections

1. Enhanced Communication: Technology allows for instant communication through various platforms like messaging apps, video calls, and social media. This makes it easier to stay in touch with friends and family, regardless of distance.

2. Access to Support Networks: Online communities and support groups can provide emotional and practical support. These platforms can be especially valuable for individuals dealing with specific challenges, such as mental health issues or chronic illnesses.

3. Opportunities for Learning and Growth: Technology provides access to a wealth of information and resources. Online courses, webinars, and discussion forums can help individuals learn new skills and expand their knowledge.

4. Facilitating Collaboration: Digital tools like project management software, collaborative documents, and virtual meeting platforms make it easier to work together on projects, whether for school, work, or personal interests.

Strategies for Leveraging Technology

1. Use Social Media Mindfully: Engage with social media in a way that enhances your well-being. Follow accounts that inspire and uplift you, and limit exposure to negative or stressful content. Use social media to connect with like-minded individuals and join groups that align with your interests.

2. Participate in Online Communities: Join forums, groups, or online communities that focus on your hobbies, interests, or professional field. These communities can provide support, advice, and a sense of belonging.

3. Schedule Regular Virtual Meetups: Use video conferencing tools to schedule regular catch-ups with friends and family. Virtual meetups can help maintain relationships and provide a sense of connection, even when in-person meetings aren't possible.

4. Leverage Educational Platforms: Take advantage of online learning platforms to acquire new skills or deepen your knowledge in areas of interest.

Practical Tips for Daily Use Set Boundaries

1. Establish clear boundaries for your technology use: Allocate specific times for checking emails, social media, and other digital activities to prevent burnout and maintain a healthy balance.

2. Stay Present: When interacting with others online, be fully present. Avoid multitasking and give your full attention to the conversation. This shows respect and fosters deeper connections.

3. Encourage Positive Interactions: Share positive content, offer support, and celebrate others' achievements. Positive interactions can create a more uplifting and supportive online environment.

Chapter 10

10.0 Future–Proofing Mental Health

Future-proofing mental health involves adopting strategies and practices that help individuals build resilience and maintain well-being in the face of future challenges. Here are some strategie to help you future-proof your mental health.

Understanding Future-Proofing Mental Health Future-proofing mental health means preparing yourself to handle future stressors and uncertainties effectively. It involves developing skills, habits, and mindsets that promote long-term mental well-being.

Key Strategies for Future-Proofing Mental Health:

1. Healthy Lifestyle Choices: Physical health and mental health are closely linked. Regular exercise, a balanced diet, adequate sleep, and hydration are essential for maintaining mental well-being. These habits can help manage stress, improve mood, and increase energy levels.

2. Continuous Learning and Adaptability: Embrace lifelong learning and be open to change. Developing new skills and staying adaptable can help you navigate future challenges more effectively. This includes both professional skills and personal development.

3. Strong Social Connections: Building and maintaining strong relationships provides emotional support and a sense of belonging. Engage in meaningful interactions with family, friends, and community members. Social support can buffer against stress and promote mental health.

4. Mindfulness and Meditation: Mindfulness practices, such as meditation, can help you stay present and reduce anxiety. Regular mindfulness practice can improve emotional regulation, increase self-awareness, and enhance overall well-being.

5. Setting Boundaries: Establishing healthy boundaries in your personal and professional life can prevent burnout and protect your mental health.

Practical Tips for Daily Life Daily Routine:

1. Establish a daily routine: Establish a daily routine includes time for self-care, relaxation, and activities you enjoy. Consistency can provide a sense of stability and control.

2. Daily Life Morning Routine: Start your day with activities that promote mental well-being, such as meditation, exercise, or a healthy breakfast.

3. Continuous Learning: Dedicate time to learning new skills or pursuing interests. This can boost your confidence and adaptability, making you better equipped to handle future challenges.

Incorporating these strategies, you can build a strong foundation for long-term mental well-being and resilience.

10.1. Adapting to Change

Adapting to change is a crucial skill for maintaining mental well-being and resilience, especially in today's fast-paced world. Here are some strategies to help you and your readers effectively adapt to change.

Understanding the Importance of Adaptability
Adaptability is the ability to adjust to new conditions and handle unexpected challenges. It involves being flexible, open-minded, and resilient in the face of change. For Generation Z, who are navigating a rapidly evolving digital landscape, academic

pressures, and social dynamics, adaptability is essential.

Benefits of Being Adaptable

1. Reduced Stress: Being adaptable helps you manage stress more effectively by allowing you to respond to changes with a positive mindset.

2. Increased Resilience: Adaptability builds resilience, enabling you to bounce back from setbacks and challenges.

3. Enhanced Problem-Solving: Adaptable individuals are better at finding creative solutions to problems and navigating complex situations.
4. Improved Relationships: Flexibility in your interactions can lead to better communication and stronger relationships.

Strategies for Developing Adaptability

1. Embrace a Growth Mindset: Adopt the belief that you can grow and improve through effort and learning. A growth mindset encourages you to view challenges as opportunities for growth rather than threats.

2. Practice Mindfulness: Mindfulness helps you stay present and focused, reducing anxiety about the future. Regular mindfulness practice can improve your ability to handle change calmly and effectively.

3. Develop Problem-Solving Skills: Enhance your problem-solving abilities by approaching challenges methodically. Break problems down into smaller, manageable parts and brainstorm potential solutions.

4. Build Emotional Intelligence: Improve your ability to recognize and manage your emotions and those of others. Emotional intelligence can help you navigate social changes and maintain positive relationships.

5. Seek Feedback: Regularly seek feedback from others to gain different perspectives and improve your adaptability. Constructive feedback can help you identify areas for growth and adjust your approach.

Practical Tips for Daily Life

1. Maintain a Positive Attitude: Focus on the positive aspects of change and the opportunities it brings. A positive attitude can make it easier to adapt and thrive.

2. Build a Support Network: Surround yourself with supportive people who can offer advice, encouragement, and different perspectives. A strong support network can help you navigate changes more effectively.

Incorporating Adaptability into Daily Life

1. Morning Routine: Start your day with activities that promote flexibility and resilience, such as meditation, exercise, or journaling.

2. Social Interactions: Practice adaptability in your social interactions by being open to different viewpoints and adjusting your communication style as needed.

10.2. Preparing for Future Challenges

Preparing for future challenges involves developing skills and strategies that enable you to navigate uncertainties and adapt to changing circumstances. Here are some detailed strategies to help readers effectively prepare for future challenges.

Understanding the Importance of Preparation

Preparation is about anticipating potential obstacles and equipping yourself with the tools and mindset needed to overcome them. For Generation Z, who face unique challenges related to technology, social dynamics, and global changes, being prepared is crucial for long-term success and well-being.

Key Strategies for Preparing for Future Challenges

1. Develop a Growth Mindset: Embrace the belief that abilities and intelligence can be developed through dedication and hard work. A growth mindset encourages resilience and a willingness to learn from experiences.

2. Enhance Problem-Solving Skills: Cultivate the ability to approach problems methodically. Break down challenges into smaller, manageable parts, and brainstorm multiple solutions. This approach helps in tackling complex issues more effectively.

3. Build Emotional Intelligence: Improve your ability to recognize, understand, and manage your emotions and those of others. High emotional intelligence can enhance relationships, reduce stress, and improve decision-making.

4. Strengthen Resilience: Resilience is the ability to bounce back from adversity. Develop resilience Maintaining a positive outlook, learning from setbacks, and staying focused on your goals.

5. Build a Support Network: Surround yourself with supportive people who can offer advice, encouragement, and different perspectives. A strong support network can help you navigate challenges more effectively.

6. Practice Mindfulness and Stress Management: Mindfulness practices, such as meditation, can help you stay present and reduce anxiety. Effective stress management techniques can improve your ability to handle future challenges calmly and efficiently.

Practical Tips for Daily Life

1. Set Realistic Goals: Establish achievable goals that allow for flexibility. This helps you stay motivated and focused, even when circumstances change.

2. Reflect and Learn: Regularly reflect on your experiences and identify what worked well and what didn't. Use these insights to inform your approach to future challenges.

3. Stay Positive: Focus on the positive aspects of change and the opportunities it brings. A positive attitude can make it easier to adapt and thrive.

Incorporating Preparation Strategies into Daily Life

1. Morning Routine: Start your day with activities that promote resilience and adaptability, such as meditation, exercise, or journaling.

2. Social Interactions: Practice adaptability in your social interactions by being open to different viewpoints and adjusting your communication style as needed.

10.3. Sustaining Mental Health Over Time

Sustaining Mental Health Over Time is not a static state but a dynamic process that requires ongoing attention and care. Sustaining mental health involves building resilience, managing stress, and maintaining a balanced lifestyle.

Key Strategies for Sustaining Mental Health

1. Regular Self-Care: Prioritise self-care activities that nourish your mind, body, and soul. This includes hobbies, relaxation techniques, and activities that bring you joy and fulfilment.

2. Healthy Lifestyle Choices: Maintain a balanced diet, exercise regularly, and get adequate sleep. Physical health is closely linked to mental health, and taking care of your body can significantly impact your mental well-being.

3. Strong Social Connections: Build and maintain strong relationships with family, friends, and community members. Social support is crucial for emotional well-being and can provide a buffer against stress.

4. Continuous Learning and Growth: Engage in lifelong learning and personal development. Acquiring new skills and knowledge can boost your confidence and adaptability, making you better equipped to handle future challenges.

5. Emotional Intelligence: Develop your emotional intelligence by improving your ability to recognize, understand, and manage your emotions and those of others. High emotional intelligence can enhance relationships and reduce stress.

Practical Tips for Daily Life Daily Routine: Establish a daily routine that includes time for self-care, relaxation, and activities you enjoy.

1. Gratitude Practice: Regularly practise gratitude by acknowledging and appreciating the positive aspects of your life. This can shift your focus from negative to positive experiences and improve your overall outlook.

2. Digital Detox: Take regular breaks from digital devices to reduce stress and improve mental clarity.

Incorporating Sustaining Strategies into Daily Life

1. Morning Routine: Start your day with activities that promote mental well-being, such as meditation, exercise, or a healthy breakfast. Allocate time for hobbies, social interactions, and relaxation to prevent burnout.

10.4. Cultivating a Growth Mindset

Cultivating a growth mindset is essential for personal development and resilience. A growth mindset, a concept introduced by psychologist Carol Dweck, is the belief that abilities and intelligence can be developed through dedication and hard work.

Benefits of a Growth Mindset Increased Resilience:

People with a growth mindset are more likely to persevere through difficulties because they see setbacks as part of the learning process.

1. Enhanced Learning: A growth mindset encourages continuous learning and improvement, leading to greater skill development and knowledge acquisition.

2. Better Problem-Solving: Viewing challenges as opportunities fosters creative problem-solving and innovation.

3. Improved Relationships: A growth mindset promotes open communication and empathy, which can strengthen personal and professional relationships.

Strategies for Cultivating a Growth Mindset

1. Embrace Challenges: Instead of avoiding difficult tasks, approach them with curiosity and a willingness to learn. Challenges are opportunities to develop new skills and knowledge.

2. Not Just Results: Focus on the effort and process rather than the outcome. Recognize and celebrate the hard work and persistence that go into achieving goals.

3. Reframe Failures as Learning Opportunities: Instead of seeing failures as a reflection of your abilities, view them as learning experiences.

4. Cultivate Curiosity: Develop a genuine interest in learning new things. Ask questions, seek out new experiences, and stay open to new ideas.

Practical Tips for Daily Life Daily Reflection

Spend a few minutes each day reflecting on what you learned and how you can apply it in the future. This practice reinforces the growth mindset.

Positive Self-Talk: Replace negative self-talk with positive affirmations. Remind yourself that you can improve with effort and persistence.

Incorporating a Growth Mindset into Daily Life

1. Morning Routine: Start your day with activities that promote a growth mindset, such as reading, journaling, or setting intentions for the day.

2. Work and Study Habits: Approach your work and studies with a focus on learning and improvement.

3. Social Interactions: Practise active listening and empathy in your interactions. Encourage others to share their experiences and learn from them.

Incorporating these strategies, you can cultivate a growth mindset that will help you navigate challenges and achieve your goals.

Conclusion

Generation Z stands at the forefront of a rapidly changing world. This book has provided practical strategies to help manage anxiety and build resilience, equipping young individuals with the tools they need to thrive. Embracing change, fostering strong support networks, prioritising mental health, and leveraging technology wisely, Generation Z can navigate the complexities of the digital age with confidence. The journey to resilience is ongoing, but with dedication and the right mindset, a brighter, more empowered future is within reach.

The digital age brings both challenges and opportunities. This book has explored ways to harness the positive aspects of technology while mitigating its potential downsides. Cultivating a growth mindset, building supportive communities, and prioritising self-care can turn anxiety into strength. The strategies outlined here are not just for overcoming obstacles but for thriving in an ever-evolving world. With these tools, Generation Z is well-prepared to face the future with resilience and optimism.

Empowering the Future Empowerment comes from within, and this book has aimed to provide the insights and strategies needed to unlock that inner strength. Generation Z, with its unique challenges and opportunities, has the potential to lead the way in creating a more resilient and connected world. Focusing on mental health, embracing continuous learning, and building strong relationships can transform anxiety into a source of power. The future is uncertain, but with the right tools and mindset, Generation Z can navigate it with confidence and grace.

Free special bonus

The Ongoing Journey of Mental Health

The journey of mental health is indeed ongoing and multifaceted. It's not a linear path but rather a series of stages and experiences that vary greatly from person to person.

Here are some key aspects to consider:

1. Awareness and Recognition: The first step in any mental health journey is recognizing that something isn't quite right. This awareness can come from personal reflection or feedback from others. It's about identifying the need for change and understanding that mental health is just as important as physical health.

2. Seeking Help: Once there's an awareness of the issue, the next step is seeking help. This can involve talking to a trusted friend or family member, consulting a mental health professional, or joining a support group. The goal is to find the right resources and support systems to begin addressing the mental health challenges.

3. Diagnosis and Treatment: Receiving a diagnosis can be a significant milestone. It provides a name for the experiences and symptoms, which can be both a relief and a challenge. It's important to remember that a diagnosis does not define a person; it's just a part of their journey

Here are more free bonus topics to consider.

Set daily screen time limit

Setting a daily screen time limit can be an effective way to manage social media usage and maintain a healthy digital balance. Here's a step-by-step guide to help you set up daily screen time limits on various devices:

For iOS devices:

1. Open the "Settings" app.
2. Tap "Screen Time."
3. Tap "App Limits," then "Add Limit."
4. Select the social media apps you want to limit, and set the desired time limit.
5. Tap "Add" to save the settings.

For Android devices:

1. Open the "Settings" app.
2. Tap "Digital Wellbeing & parental controls."
3. Tap "Dashboard" to view your app usage.
4. Set the desired time limit and tap "OK."

For computers and laptops:

1. Install a browser extension or third-party app like RescueTime or Cold Turkey, which can help you track your usage and set daily limits for social media sites.

Setting a daily screen time limit can help you create a healthier relationship with social media and reduce its potential impact on your mental health.

Social media overload

Social media overload refers to the excessive use of social media platforms, which can lead to negative effects on mental health. Some of these impacts include:

1. **Anxiety and depression:** Constantly comparing oneself to others and the fear of missing out can trigger or worsen anxiety and depression symptoms.

2. **Sleep disturbance:** Spending prolonged periods on social media, especially before bedtime, can affect sleep quality and lead to insomnia.

3. **Addiction and obsession:** Overuse of social media can create an unhealthy dependence, resulting in obsessive behaviours such as constantly checking for notifications.

4. Low self-esteem: Exposure to idealised images and lifestyles on social media can lower self-esteem and increase body image issues.

5. Cyberbullying and online harassment: Experiencing or witnessing negative interactions on social media can contribute to stress and feelings of vulnerability.

Try a 10-minute guided meditation.
A 10-minute guided meditation can be a great way to cultivate mindfulness, reduce stress, and enhance your overall well-being. Here are the steps to follow:

1. Set aside 10 minutes for a guided meditation session.

2. Choose a comfortable and quiet location where you won't be disturbed.

3. Select a guided meditation resource, such as an audio recording, video, or mobile app.

4. Sit or lie down in a comfortable position, allowing your body to relax.

5. Follow the instructions provided by the guided meditation, focusing on your breath, body, and surroundings.

6. Notice any thoughts, emotions, or sensations that arise, acknowledging them without judgment.

7. Allow the calming voice to lead you through the meditation, helping you become more present and relaxed.

8. After the 10 minutes have passed, gently bring your awareness back to your surroundings.

9. Reflect on the experience and notice any changes in your mental or emotional state.

Egaging in this 10-minute guided meditation practice, you can enjoy numerous benefits, such as increased relaxation, improved concentration, and enhanced well-being.

Explore breathing exercises.
Breathing exercises can be a powerful tool for managing stress, improving focus, and enhancing your overall well-being. Here are some popular breathing techniques to explore:

1. Diaphragmatic breathing: Breathe deeply into your diaphragm, expanding your belly as you inhale and contracting it as you exhale.

2. Box breathing: Inhale for a count of four, hold for four, exhale for four, and pause for four. Repeat this pattern for several cycles to promote relaxation and improve focus.

3. Alternate nostril breathing: Breathe in through one nostril, hold your breath, then breathe out through the opposite nostril. Repeat this pattern, alternating nostrils with each cycle, to balance the left and right hemispheres of the brain.

4. Progressive muscle relaxation: Tense and release different muscle groups in your body while focusing on your breath. This helps release tension and promote relaxation throughout your body.

5. 4-7-8 breathing: Breathe in for four counts, hold for seven counts, and exhale for eight counts.

Create a personalized coping toolkit.
Creating a personalized coping toolkit can help you manage stress and maintain mental well-being.

1. Identify your stress triggers: Recognize situations, people, or events that cause stress for you. This will help you anticipate when to use your coping tools.

2. Choose your coping tools: Experiment with different stress-management techniques, such as deep breathing, meditation, exercise, journaling, or creative activities. Find the ones that work best for you and make you feel more relaxed and centered.

3. Make a list: Write down your preferred coping tools and keep the list accessible, such as in your wallet, on your phone, or in a journal.

4. Organize your toolkit: Categorize your coping tools based on the level of stress or the time you have available to use them.

Unfollow accounts that contribute to anxiety.

Unfollowing accounts that contribute to anxiety can help reduce your exposure to negative content and promote better mental health. Here are some tips for identifying and unfollowing these accounts:

1. Pay attention to your emotions: Notice how certain accounts make you feel. If you find yourself feeling anxious, stressed, or unhappy after viewing their content, it may be time to unfollow.

2. Look for patterns: Identify themes or types of content that tend to trigger negative emotions for you.

3. Assess your news sources: Consider unfollowing or limiting exposure to news outlets that consistently report on distressing events or use sensational headlines.

4. Unfollow toxic people: If you have friends or acquaintances who post content that consistently makes you feel anxious or upset, it's okay to unfollow them or mute their posts.

5. Follow uplifting accounts: Replace the negative accounts with ones that promote positivity, self-care, and mental well-being.

Bing more selective about the accounts you follow, you can create a more supportive and nurturing online environment for yourself.

Dear Reader,

Thank you for joining us on this journey through "Generation Z: Empowering the Anxious Generation." Your time and attention mean the world to me.

As an author, I believe that the true magic lies in the connections we create through words. Your insights, experiences, and reflections matter immensely. Whether you found solace, inspiration, or a fresh perspective within these pages, I'd love to hear from you.

Would you kindly consider leaving a review. Your honest feedback not only helps other readers discover this book but also fuels my passion to continue writing meaningful content.

Remember, your voice matters. Let's build a community of resilience together one review at a time.